Reprints of Economic Classics

Veblen

BY AND ABOUT VEBLEN
Available in Reprints of Economic Classics

IMPERIAL GERMANY
And the Industrial Revolution (1915). With an Introduction by Joseph Dorfman (1939)

AN INQUIRY INTO THE NATURE OF PEACE
And the Terms of Its Perpetuation (1917)

THE VESTED INTERESTS
And the Common Man. "The Modern Point of View and the New Order"

THE INSTINCT OF WORKMANSHIP
And the State of the Industrial Arts (1922) With an Introductory Note by Joseph Dorfman

ABSENTEE OWNERSHIP
And Business Enterprise in Recent Times The Case of America (1923)

ESSAYS IN OUR CHANGING ORDER
(A Posthumous Collection of Papers from Periodicals) Edited by Leon Ardzrooni (1934)

WHAT VEBLEN TAUGHT
Selected Writings of Thorstein Veblen with an Introduction by Wesley C. Mitchell (1936)

THORSTEIN VEBLEN AND HIS AMERICA
By Joseph Dorfman (1934)

VEBLEN
By John A. Hobson (1936)

VEBLEN

By
J. A. HOBSON

REPRINTS OF ECONOMIC CLASSICS

Augustus M. Kelley, Bookseller
New York 1963

First published 1936

CONTENTS

		PAGE
	Preface	9
CHAPTER		
I.	Thorstein Veblen	11
II.	The Place of Economics in the Sciences	23
III.	Veblen's attitude towards Marx	53
IV.	Veblen's Socialism	66
V.	Social implications of a Predatory System	87
VI.	The Economics of Education	104
VII.	The Field of Politics	121
VIII.	Personal Prestige	164
IX.	A Summary and Estimate	183
	Index	225

PREFACE

THORSTEIN VEBLEN is only known to a limited class of English readers by his *Theory of a Leisure Class* which, though rightly representative of his distinctive sociology, by no means does full justice to the depth of his research into and the acuteness of his interpretation of the origin and development of social institutions under the dominant pressure of economic forces. My attempt here is to give an intelligible account of Veblen's various approaches, anthropological, biological, psychological, that converge in his economic determination of the history of his time and country. No American sociologist has brought a wider intellectual equipment, a keener brain and a more objective vision to bear upon the spectacle of American social processes and institutions, and possibly because America has in some respects outrun the economic pace of other civilized countries, Veblen's analysis should have a special value in helping us to forecast our own economic future.

In the space at my disposal I have not been able to do full justice to the breadth of Veblen's treatment in discussing the relations between the economic and the non-economic factors in social evolution. Many of my readers will, I hope, be encouraged to read the large volume by Joseph Dorfman, entitled *Thorstein Veblen and his America*, which gives a full and able account of Veblen's teaching, and upon which I have drawn freely not only for the brief story of his life in my opening chapter, but for the interpretation of some difficult passages in his writings.

J. A. HOBSON.

January, 1936.

CHAPTER I

THORSTEIN VEBLEN

NO study of Veblen's sociology would be intelligible without some account of his personality and career. This is true, no doubt, of every active worker in those sciences which touch personal and social activities. But it has a special application to the case of one of the great thinkers of our age whose thought, as exhibited in his writings, is so powerfully penetrated by the distinctive personal experience of his American environment. Veblen's thinking, for reasons which will be intelligible when we study it, never received much attention outside a small intellectual circle, even in his own country, and in England he is almost unknown among students of the social sciences, with the exception of a small company acquainted with his *The Theory of a Leisure Class* which they are apt to regard more as satire than as science, because they are unfamiliar with the American situation in its modern evolution.

The first point of significance in Veblen's life history is a certain independence and aloofness of attitude towards the American people and their institutions, due to his foreign origin. Born in 1857 of Norwegian stock, farmer immigrants into Wisconsin, Veblen spent his first seventeen years in a self-sufficient farmstead, which in its home life and its work preserved the character of rural Norway. The language and cultural interests remained those of Scandinavia, and they had practically no social intercourse with their English-speaking neighbours. Though English was taught and spoken in the public schools, it was ignored outside in the home, the Church and the playtime. Thorstein was the sixth child of a family of twelve. His father was a stubborn, taciturn, thoughtful but slow-witted man, his mother endowed with remarkable qualities of character. "It was from her that Thorstein got his personality and brains."[1]

His father, deciding that Thorstein was suited for the Lutheran ministry, dispatched him at the age of seventeen to Carleton College Academy. Here he was plunged into a line of study taken over from the New England colleges, in which religion and moral philosophy were mingled with a study of the classics and a tincture of mathematics with a little botany and zoology, but no serious attempt at scientific teaching in the modern sense. "The Moral Philosophy" taught, "that the desire to possess, to

[1] Dorfman, p. 11.

appropriate, lies among the native and implanted principles of the soul," and that, "Man has not only the right to life and liberty, but also to *property*, or the possession and enjoyment of whatever he may, by his own industry or good fortune, or the gift of others, have honestly acquired."[1]

Such Political Economy as was taught conformed to this common-sense philosophy, and we can see how the challenge would be taken up by the free powerful mind of young Veblen. The agrarianism of the Middle-West was beginning to assert itself in conflict with the new railroad dominion and the money-lenders of the country towns, the packers and middlemen who handled farm produce and its prices.

Veblen, always a realist in the basis of his thinking, naturally discovered a sharp contrast between the "natural rights" theories of his philosophical and economic textbooks and the hard facts of the social-economic life with which he was familiar. But this was only one factor in his intellectual awakening. His mind spread itself profusely among the liberal philosophers and social thinkers available in the library, most of them outside the limits of the lecture room. Kant, Spencer, Mill, Hume, Voltaire, Huxley appealed to different strains of interest in him, and he began a study of Old Norse

[1] Op. cit., p. 21.

and its literature, together with the modern languages which his fine memory enabled him to absorb with ease as by-products of his more serious studies.

Neither the faculty nor his fellow-students showed much liking for this queer youth. He seemed incapable of making friends in the ordinary social sense of the term. But, in every stage of his career, he won the admiration of one or more serviceable allies. At Carleton Professor John Bates Clark, a liberal economist, though not on Veblen's lines, became a lifelong friend and stood by him on many occasions when his "radicalism" was vigorously assailed.

His public oration on graduation day did not, however, indicate a sociological career. Its subject was "Mill's Examination of Hamilton's Philosophy of the Conditioned." But his earliest post as a teacher was neither in philosophy nor economics, but in mathematics. For a year he taught in a Norwegian college in Madison, Wisconsin. When this college failed, Thorstein with a brother found his way to Johns Hopkins in Baltimore where philosophy at first continued to be his chief study. Failing to obtain a scholarship that would provide him with a living, he then turned to Yale, again with the purpose of studying philosophy. Continually hampered by financial difficulties, he managed to struggle through for two and a half years to his degree in 1884, with a dissertation upon "Ethical Grounds of a Doctrine of Retribution." Failing to obtain any acceptable teaching post, he returned to the farm settlement of his family and loafed and read for the next few years, writing a few articles which remained unpublished, and talking over economic and political problems with his father. This was the time when the growing grievances of the farmers evoked the Farmers' Alliance, while Henry George made his popular appeal for the Single Tax, and anarchism raised it head in the bombing at Chicago. Economic issues were forcing their way into a wider public attention, and liberal economists, Richard Ely and J. B. Clark at their head, were grouping themselves in the American Economic Association, with what was regarded by the older school as a "socialistic" tendency.

Veblen, in his bucolic retirement took no part in these movements, though following them with keen interest. With characteristic recklessness he married in 1888 the bright educated daughter of an Iowa farmer whom he had known as a Carleton fellow-student. After further failure to get a college teaching-post, he registered as a student at Cornell in 1891, passing from history and law into the economics department then in charge of

Professor J. L. Laughlin. Spencer's *Plea for Liberty* was then stirring controversy in American intellectual circles, and Veblen opened his distinctively sociological writings with an elaborate discussion of this essay, entitled *Some Neglected Points in the Theory of Socialism*. Obtaining a fellowship at Cornell, Veblen with his wife settled down there for a year during which he published several economic articles, discussing the wage-fund doctrine, Böhm Bawerk and *The Overproduction Fallacy*. The next year, 1892, he followed Professor Laughlin to Chicago as a lecturer in economics and had his first experience of a great industrial centre. His age was now forty-five and he was at the beginning of his economic career as writer and teacher.

It is needless to follow closely his subsequent activities which are accurately recorded in his output of articles and books in which economics figures as the basis of other social studies. For some years he was busily engaged in teaching small classes and in publishing articles for the *Journal*. It was not until 1899 that his first book *The Theory of the Leisure Class, an Economic Study in the Evolution of Institutions* saw the light of day, marking the distinctive line of his sociology. Its popularity among radicals was chiefly due to its satirical commentary upon the upper classes, rather than to its scientific exposition of the facts of the American situation. In 1900 he was promoted to the rank of assistant professor. This year began an era of sensational exposures of "high finance and corrupt politics"[1] in which, however, Veblen took no personal part. He was more deeply concerned with two books which absorbed his attention, Ward's *Pure Sociology* and Sombart's *Der Moderne Capitalismus* in which he saw the beginnings of a genuinely scientific spirit applied to social changes, and a recognition of the vital distinction between industry and business. Having now more money at his disposal, Veblen made several visits to Europe, where he moved in the company of artists and scientists and attractive women. Partly from sheer restlessness, partly from marital disagreements, he was impelled to leave Chicago and find other occupation. But, though he had influential personal backing, he failed to obtain the post of chief librarian in the Library of Congress, for which he applied in 1904, was rejected as a proposed member of the Harvard faculty, and was eventually invited by President David Starr Jordan to a post at Leland Stanford University in California.

There he stayed for three years, teaching economics to small classes of undergraduates who were not easily attuned to his methods and

[1] Op. cit., p. 209.

manners. His knowledge was encyclopædic but his attempts to impart it were singularly ineffective, partly from the disorderly method of his talk, partly from sheer physical defects. Even his ironic humour faded in his classes, and his brilliance of analysis failed to shine in this academic environment.

It was not, however, so much these teaching defects as "personal affairs" that caused him to resign his work at Stanford. Then, after various unsuccessful applications at Toronto and elsewhere, Veblen seems to have devoted himself chiefly to papers which formed the substance of a volume entitled *The Higher Learning in America*, and spent some time in retirement in Idaho. His friend H. J. Davenport, head of the economic department at the University of Missouri, then secured for him a lectureship and, from 1911 to the Great War, he led an uneasy life in Columbia, at a meagre salary, suffering much from ill health and more from chronic dissatisfaction with his social environment. When the Great War broke out, Veblen was travelling in Norway where he obtained a recognition as a great man which he found very pleasing. Returning to his teaching post in Columbia he produced a book on *Imperial Germany* dealing not with the War itself but with the political economic evolution which made the War inevitable. Shortly after Wilson's election to the Presidency he began writing *An Inquiry into the Nature of Peace and the Terms of its Perpetuation*, in which he set out the thesis that business enterprise is the directive force in the modern sovereign State and the main source of dynastic ambition and patriotic fervour. Permanent peace is only attainable either by complete submission to the imperial State or by the elimination of business enterprise in its modern pecuniary shape.

When America came into the War, Colonel House was instructed to prepare a Memorandum upon the terms of a possible peace settlement, and Veblen was invited to take part in its preparation. His chief contribution *An Outline of a Policy for the Control of the Economic Penetration of Backward Countries and of Foreign Investments* indicates how far his mind was working in advance of the practical statesmanship of his time. His work was given no prominence in the report of the House Inquiry for reasons intelligible enough when its far-reaching implications are realized.

In June 1918 Veblen was appointed one of the Editors of *The Dial* and moved to New York. A series of his articles was published in book form early in 1919 under the title *The Vested Interests and the State of the Industrial Arts*. The support of influential liberals in the *New Republic*, the *Nation* and other radical journals hoisted Veblen on to a pinnacle of temporary fame as the prophet of his time. Veblenists and Veblen Clubs acquired a vogue.[1] But it is difficult in America for fame to dispense with some of those personal factors in which Veblen was so deficient. He could not "orate," he would not even talk to order or to expectation. As Dorfman says of him, "His protective mechanism of silence had become his master."[2] Nor can it be supposed that articles imputed to him in *The Dial*, representing Bolshevism as a menace to the Vested Interests, would help his reputation in any quarter but the negligible communists. The "Red Terror" which swept over America in 1919–20, in which Socialists, Pacifists, Internationalists, Communists were subjected to all sorts of legal and illegal violence, drove such argumentation as that of Veblen into almost complete neglect. The gallant attempt to associate him with the establishment of the "New School for Social Research" which was "to seek an unbiased understanding of the existing order" and in which a number of Veblen's friends and admirers took part was of little lasting service to him. For his inability to hold the students attracted by his reputation soon became apparent. His position became precarious, and after the changes in the structure of "The New School" in 1922, he was driven to seek a new teach-

[1] Op. cit., p. 420.   [2] Op. cit., p. 424.

ing post. An attempt to organize technicians into an alliance for the furtherance of their control of industry failed to win the necessary support, and the brief notoriety of a movement of Technology a few years later was subjected to such severe criticism in liberal as well as conservative quarters as to damage the practical reputation of the Veblenist position. The title of Veblen's last book *Absentee Ownership* denotes the strong persistence of his distinctive contribution to the brand of economic determinism assumed thirty years before. But by 1927 his failing health drove him back to Palo Alto to pass his last years in weakness and in poverty, relieved only by the contributions of one or two well-to-do friends. His death occurred in August 1929 in his seventy-third year. Had he lived to see the great depression which began in the next year, his grim humour might have felt a certain satisfaction in the *debâcle* of that finance which he held responsible for all modern economic maladies. This thought finds expression in a statement made in 1934 by his great admirer Stuart Chase. "Thorstein Veblen, the greatest economist this country has produced, died in obscurity a few years ago. Day by day as the depression deepens, the soundness of his analysis, the awful import of his prophecy, becomes more apparent. It is a pity that he should not have been spared to witness, a faint sardonic smile upon his lips, the brood of black ravens which have come to roost."[1]

It would not, however, do justice to Veblen's mind and work to dwell overmuch upon this testimony to his prophetic genius or the humour which sometimes accompanied his literary expression. He was essentially a powerful exploratory thinker, his economic and sociological teaching being based upon deep philosophical and psychological studies which gave him a fuller understanding of human personality and society than any other of his countrymen. Though his thinking, as that of others, was influenced and even directed by the external circumstances of his upbringing and environment, he was always able to take an objective view of those very factors and thereby to preserve a freedom and veracity that enabled him to discover and reveal the structure of modern society and some of its operative tendencies more truthfully than any other thinker of his age.

[1] Quoted Dorfman, p. 509.

CHAPTER II

THE PLACE OF ECONOMICS IN THE SCIENCES

THE volume in which Veblen digs deepest into the roots of his social-economic teaching is entitled *The Place of Science in Modern Civilization*. Beginning with an inquiry into the origins of science, as disclosed by anthropological accounts of the working of the mind of primitive man, he lays stress on the distinction between the disorderly knowledge of concrete facts of a directly pragmatic or utilitarian character, acquired in the necessary processes of getting food, shelter and other biological requirements, and the interpretation of these facts and the nature of environment under the urge of disinterested mental activity, or what he prefers to call "idle curiosity." These two sources of science he envisages as separate and opposed in their nature and early operation. "Idle curiosity," he thinks, may be closely related to the aptitude for play in man and in the lower animals, an activity that "seems peculiarly lively in the young, whose aptitude for sustained pragmatism is at the same time relatively vague and unreliable." (p. 7.)

Among savages and primitive men the interpretation of facts under the guidance of "idle curiosity" generally takes shape in anthropomorphic or animistic explanations of the conduct of the objects regarded as agents. This animism inspires the myths and legends which come to have a high superstitious value in primitive societies, the crude beginnings of philosophy. As "idle curiosity" becomes more comprehensive in its sweep and closer in its observation, its dramatic cosmology becomes less crudely animistic, though retaining the broad general principle of generation. "Procreation, birth, growth and decay constitute the cycle of postulates within which the dramatized processes of natural phenomena run their course." (p. 9).

Physical causation has only a secondary and an obscure part in such intellectual play. The ordinary vulgar work and life processes are, of course, realized usually in terms of natural causation, but these terms do not yet manifest themselves as "laws" or enter any claim to furnish rules of conduct. Veblen distinguishes this early stage where "the ruling institutions are those of blood relationship, descent and clannish discrimination" from the subsequent cultural era of the Middle Ages when "graded dignity, authenticity and dependence" are the canons of social life. "Natural laws are corollaries under the arbitrary rules of status imposed on the natural universe by an all-powerful Providence with a view to the maintenance of His own prestige. The Science that grows in such a spiritual environment is of the class represented by alchemy and astrology, in which the imputed degrees of nobility and prepotency of the objects and the symbolic force of their names are looked to for an explanation of what takes place." (p. 12).

So long as a community is organized upon a coercive basis with well-marked ruling and subject classes, these two sources of knowledge and interpretation will remain distinct. The higher theoretical knowledge with its more speculative generalizations will stand aloof from the humbler sorts of ordered skill and information which belong to workmanlike efficiency.

A distinction, however, is found between the peaceable agricultural communities, where the laws of nature impose themselves upon the ordinary behaviour of the environment, expressing themselves "in terms of generation or germination and growth," and the more predatory life of pastoral peoples which demands a more arbitrary and centralized authority. The former type is likely to manifest a poly-theistic theology related to the varied powers of nature each of which needs special study and conciliation. "The relation of the deities to mankind is likely to be that of consanguinity, and as if to emphasize the peaceable non-coercive character of the divine order of things the deities are, in the main, very apt to be females. The matters of interest dealt with in the cosmological theories are chiefly matters of the livelihood of the people, the growth and care of the crops, and the promotion of industrial ways and means." (p. 47).

Very different will be the cosmology and theology of a pastoral people with definitely predatory habits. Such a people will make their religions conform to their earthly habits of leadership and energy. They will tend to a monotheistic, arbitrary scheme of divine government. Their explanations will be in terms of an arbitrary fiat. "Such a people will adopt male deities, in the main, and will impute to them a coercive, imperious, arbitrary animus and a degree of princely dignity." (p. 48).

Right from the earliest times we thus perceive the directive influence of economic conditions upon human thinking and the political and religious institutions which arise from the combined needs for organized power and the play of creative speculation. But it is not until the work-a-day knowledge has advanced further in technological efficiency (so that the effective control of the environment for human uses has become well established), that industry begins to enter and to dominate other departments of social life, impressing its needs upon law and politics and weakening the reign of the old clan distinctions.

Here Veblen thrusts into the foreground of his social theory the factor of technological advance. In this way science leaves its early path of speculative inquiry with a religious bias and comes under the sway of "efficient cause" as evidenced in the practical experience of working activities. "In this way, it may be conceived, modern science came into the field under the cloak of technology and gradually encroached on the domain of authentic theory previously held by other, higher, nobler, more profound, more spiritual, more intangible conceptions and theories of knowledge. In this early phase of modern science its central norm and universal solvent is the concept of workmanlike initiative and efficiency." (p. 50).

In this account of the advance of economic determinism Veblen is careful to limit its early influence to the inorganic sciences and in particular to exclude from its direct control, ethics, political science and economics, though, as we shall see later on, the social sciences are indirectly but even more effectively influenced by changes in the economic activities and structure than are the physical sciences. Indeed, though the physical sciences were delivered from the vagaries of a speculative play of the mind and set upon a sound inductive basis by the requirements of the new industrial mentality with its demand for ordered facts and linked explanations, it is not claimed that the sciences were directly evolved to serve the utilitarian ends of the industrial arts. The organized curiosity of the sciences still remains "idle" in that devoted scientists insist upon free play for their minds in the pursuance of knowledge which is not to be valued on any utilitarian standard and only affords help to the practical services by its by-products. How far this free play is, however, itself, regulated or modified by the secret play of gainful motives, is a question only to be answered by Veblen later on in the more detailed examination of his economic determinism.

It must here suffice to recognize the profound changes in methods of thinking produced by the change-over from handicraft technology to the machine and power methods of the Industrial Revolution. The entire social and cultural attitudes of common life, brought about by the work and life of mines, factories and organized trade, with their financial apparatus, are, indeed, too obvious to require citation. The work of intellectual and moral transformation is not, however, by any means completed. "The metaphysics of the machine technology have not yet wholly, perhaps not mainly, superseded the metaphysics of the code

PLACE OF ECONOMICS IN THE SCIENCES

of honour in those lines of inquiry that have to do with human initiative and aspiration. Whether such a shifting shall ever be effected is still an open question. Here there still are spiritual verities which transcend the sweep of consecutive change. That is to say, there are still earnest habits of thought which definitely predispose their hearers to bring their inquiries to rest on grounds of differential quality and invidious merit." (p. 55).

The illusiveness of these final terms for most readers serves to illustrate certain qualities of Veblen's thought and expression which throughout his life impeded the recognition of his intellectual achievements. While perceiving clearly enough the limits of his technological explanation of cultural changes outside the economic field, he is loth to give them a genuine independence. Though from time to time he qualifies his central theory, he does so grudgingly and with evasive explanations.

Most sociologists will hold that his technological factor is overstressed as a transforming medium. Though machinery has undoubtedly influenced our ways of thinking and our attitude to the services, it has been less revolutionary than Veblen is disposed to think. The machine-tender is not much more the slave of routine than were the main body of handicraftsmen, and the proportion of machine-tenders is continually diminishing in favour of machine-rulers in mines, factories, railways and other industries employing machine-power. Most men employ their thinking processes on subjects that really interest them and an increasing number of these subjects lie outside the shorter work-day of most modern workers. Home life, sport and other recreations bulk bigger in most lives, and though the work for livelihood must count considerably as a secret moulder of character and mentality, it does not predominate.

It is true that in the expanding field of leisure occupations the elaboration of machinery plays an increasing part. The motor-car, the cinema and the radio, have in a single generation produced what alarmists term a mechanization of the leisure mind. Formerly, we are told, it was the mechanical control over the producer that encroached upon his liberty; now it is the mechanical control of the consumer. The problem of deciding whether this process of mechanization creates more liberty than it takes away is not an easy one. Even the substitution of motor-car or cycle for the horse, as a mode of transport, does not necessarily imply a curtailment of skilled control for the traveller. His contacts with his mechanical carrier are more those of the skilled mechanical ruler rather than of the servile instrument, and the enlarged mobility of his journeying must count on the side of increased freedom. A more specious case is made for the centralized Press, the school, the cinema and the radio, as instruments for imposed conformity of thoughts and feelings. Some modern instances, indeed, disclose a peril of a novel type when centralized control of the machinery of propaganda is brought to bear upon a submissive and recipient public mind. Since all creative progress comes from the assertive intelligence of single minds with free access to the avenues of information, the seizure of these avenues by dictators or ruling minorities, determined to form the thoughts and emotions of the multitude after the single pattern of their interests and needs, would seem to involve the stoppage of free thought not merely in politics, economics, morals and religion, but in all the arts and sciences which go to the building and maintenance of a civilization. Whether this peril can be met depends in part upon the strength of the natural resistance of the educated mind to dictated doctrine. It is not so easy to secure uniformity of imposed belief and conduct in a people whose traditions carry a sense and an obligation of free-thinking and personal valuations, as in groups of primitive men whose personality has not emerged from the stage of authoritarian chief-worship with its superstitious implications. But this is not the only source of resistance to the attempted mechanization of the mind. The stoppage of free-thought in its application to the social arts and sciences cannot fail to react upon all other applications of a maimed mentality. The free exploratory impulse will disappear from the physical sciences and the technology of industry will itself suffer decay and obsolescence. In short, a contradiction will be disclosed in the technique of tyranny, ultimately expressed in a loss of the force upon which it relies for its dominion. In terms of politics a completely despotic State, exercising a mechanical dominion over the minds and bodies of its people would, on the one hand, fail to satisfy the most urgent material needs of that people, and, on the other hand, would lose that progressive control over the technology of force required for its survival in the international arena.

. . . . .

The foregoing considerations indicate that Veblen favours in a large measure what is termed the economic interpretation of history by stressing the influence of technological advances and the Industrial Revolution upon other aspects of human life and the sciences which deal with them. The fuller discussion of his "economic interpretation" must, however, be deferred until we have disentangled from his various presentations of the issue a clearer understanding of his criticisms of current economic science.

His more formal criticism is best presented in an article entitled "Why is Economics not an evolutionary science?" published in 1898,[1] and in three articles on "The Preconceptions of Economic Science" which appeared in the following year.[2] Some of the terminology which he feels constrained to use is so unusual as to make readers uncertain how far they have grasped his meaning.[3] Economics and the other social sciences have, he maintains, failed to keep pace with the physical sciences in adopting the evolutionary method of a dispassionate cumulative causation in the sequence of events. "Economics—shows too many reminiscences of the 'natural' and the 'normal,' of 'verities' and 'tendencies' of 'controlling principles' and 'disturbing causes' to be classed as an evolutionary science." "This history of the science shows a long and devious course of disintegrating animism—from the days of the scholastic writers

---

[1] *Quarterly Journal of Economics*, Vol. XII, July, 1898.
[2] *Quarterly Journal of Economics*, June, July, October, 1899.
[3] One difficulty with Veblen is his semi-humorous recourse to cryptic utterances, feigning that they are explanatory. An example may be quoted from p. 70: "But what does all this signify? If we are getting restless under the taxonomy of a monocotyledonous wage-system and cryptogamic theory of interest, with involute, loculicidal, tomentous and monoliform variants, what is the cytoplasm, centrosome, or karyokinetic process to which we may turn, and in which we may find surcease from the metaphysics of normality and controlling principles."

who discussed money from the point of view of its relation to the divine suzerainty, to the Physiocrats who rested their case on an '*ordre naturel*' and a '*loi naturelle*' that decides what is substantially true, and, in a general way, guides the course of events by the constraint of logical consequence."[1]

So too in the classical political economy from Adam Smith to Mill and Cairnes the guidance of an "invisible hand" gradually gave way to less providential views of "natural" wages and "normal" value. This treatment of economic process is considered pre-evolutionary because it rests upon what Veblen terms a "taxonomic" treatment, as opposed to the dynamic treatment demanded by the evolutionary conception. The central assumption of this "taxonomy" appears in the acceptance of a tendency to equilibrium at the normal, involving a belief in the continued rightness of a system of checks and balances which, when the equilibrium is disturbed, tend to its restoration. Such a system is found in the theories of "cost of production," "iron law of wages," "limitation of industry by capital," "the law of interest" which seemed to be the chief regulative principles of early-nineteenth century capitalism.

Though Cairnes, and later Marshall, were restive under the Ricardian rule and effected con-

[1] *The Plan of Science*, p. 64.

siderable improvements in the formulation of the economic "laws," they were prevented by adherence to certain earlier preconceptions from proceeding far towards the evolutionary requirements of a science of cumulative change corresponding to the requirements of the changing arts of industry.

Neither the economic theorists nor the historical school have endeavoured to make their science "a genetic account of the economic life process."[1] The reason for this failure, Veblen holds, is to be found mainly in the adoption from the Benthamite utilitarianism of a definitely hedonist psychology and a refusal to abandon it when it has been displaced by modern psychological analysis.

Even when J. S. Mill in effect destroyed this utilitarian calculus by admitting qualities as well as quantities in pleasure and pain, the convenience of a science ever striving towards quantitative exactitude retained the early interpretation of economic motives. Though modern psychology and modern anthropology have expelled hedonism from its authoritative post as the explanation of human activity, it still retains its position in the economic calculus.

It is a pity that in handling this critical question of motive Veblen does not enter more closely into an analysis of the complex relations of human

[1] Op. cit., p. 72.

urges, instincts, or nisus to activity. He is too content with such a general setting of his case as the following: "According to this conception, it is the characteristic of man to do something, not simply to suffer pleasures and pains through the import of suitable causes. He is *not merely a bundle of desires that are to be saturated by being placed in the path of the forces of the environment, but rather a coherent structure of propensities and habits* which seek realization and expression in an unfolding activity."[1] Now the phrases here italicized demand a fuller examination than they here receive. For, though the crude hedonism which presents man as consciously impelled to all actions by a desire to win a definite pleasure, or to avoid a definite pain, is clearly indefensible, it by no means follows that such utilitarianism as that of J. S. Mill and some of the later economists must be rejected. For what is this "coherent structure of propensities and habits which seeks realization and expression" apart from the conscious satisfaction of attainment? Propensities and habits are not created by chance or in the void: they are ultimately rooted in biological utilities, and the pleasurable emotions which accompany their activities are not separable from such activities and may be taken as true registers of those utilities, whether those utilities are confined to the demands

[1] Op. cit., p. 71.

of biological survival or include other elements of personal self-realization and progress.

It is necessary to qualify the downright repudiation of Hedonism in Veblen's analysis by this more liberal assertion of the element of conscious satisfaction in all human achievement, because, when we come to his concrete interpretation of modern evolutionary society, we shall perceive that the conscious striving after prestige and power as testimony to economic success occupies the centre of the modern social-economic stage.

His repudiation of Hedonism, as it appears in the early classical economics, is designed to correct what he held to be the two basic falsehoods of the "natural" economy of a taxonomic system, to which reference has already been made under the title of "animism" and "equilibrium." For long after the abandonment of Adam Smith's assertion that man, though always consciously seeking his own gain, is "led as by an invisible hand to promote an end which was no part of his intention," the individualist's direct concern with his definite personal gain is given as a warrant for the social good proceeding from the play of competition in industry. When to this interpretation is added the belief that there exists in this competitive struggle a "natural" tendency to defeat all interferences and to overcome all friction, in order to restore the equilibrium which forms the necessary condition of a sound economic order, the significance of what Veblen terms the taxonomic preconception as opposed to the dynamic is made manifest.

As economic science advanced, both these supports for a "natural" economy weakened. But while "the invisible hand" may be said to have disappeared and the "equilibrium" has lost much of its static significance and taken on a changeful and progressive character, economic science retains certain features of the pre-evolutionary thought. The most important of these features relates to the theory of value. Though it was always formally recognized that the welfare or satisfaction of consumers was the end and object of all productive processes, little attention was given to standards of consumption as affected either by the character of goods produced or by their quantitative distribution. All attention was absorbed in considering the processes of production, for the very nature of these processes, it was held, determined the distribution and the consumption of wealth. This statement seems at first sight contradicted by the professed claims of some early classical economists. Ricardo, for example, formally insisted upon the dominant character of distribution. "The produce of the earth—all that is derived from its surface by the united application of labour, machinery and capital, is divided among three classes of the community. ... To determine the laws which regulate this distribution, is the principal problem of political economy."[1]

But, when we come to the consideration of the laws which regulate this distribution, we find them expressed in certain natural laws and fixed human motives operative in the processes of production.

The law of rent determines the share which goes to the landowner, the more or less "iron" law of wages the share that goes to labour, while the rate of interest regulates the amount of savings and consequently the share that goes to capital. Though many of the classical economists admitted modifications in the rigour of those laws, the problem of distribution, as a whole, was rooted in the necessities of the productive processes: the wants of man and his sense of an equitable and humanly desirable distribution found no definite plan in the classic scheme.

And yet, apart from the factor of rent, the distributive process, as envisaged by the classical economists, retained an element of "natural" justice operative through the play of hedonist motives. Veblen thus expresses it: "In hedonistic theory the substantial end of economic life is individual gain; and for this purpose production and acquisition may be taken as fairly coincident, if

[1] Preface. *Political Economy.*

not identical. Moreover, Society, in the utilitarian philosophy, is the algebraic sum of the individuals; and the interest of the Society is the sum of the interests of the individual. It follows by easy consequence, whether strictly true or not, that the sum of individual gains is the gain of the society, and that, in serving his own interest in the way of acquisition, the individual serves the collective interest of the community. Productivity or serviceability is, therefore, to be presumed of any occupation or enterprise that looks to a pecuniary gain; and so, by a roundabout path we get back to the ancient conclusion of Adam Smith, that the remuneration of classes or persons engaged in industry coincides with their productive contribution to the output of services and consumable goods."[1]

Though rent is not the remuneration for any personal services of the landowner, it is payment commensurate with the productivity of the land which is his legal property. Apart from this, the payments in money or in goods made to the providers of capital and the various classes of brain and hand workers, under an economy of easy mobility and equality of opportunity, would "naturally" correspond to their individual productive services. Though there is some confusion due to the use of the term "profit" and the part its recipient plays as

[1] *The Plan of Science*, p. 139.

residual legatee, while "wages of superintendence" are apt to be fused with interest and profit in the earlier capital system, such difficulties are not allowed to override the general conclusion that every contributor to production tends to get what he is "worth" in terms of the size of his contribution.[1]

Now, though later on when Jevons came into the field, productive contributions came to be reckoned in consumptive utility rather than in productive costs, the "cost" theory on the whole prevailed because of its closer relation to the "scarcity" basis of valuation. For without "scarcity" no values in the economic sense can emerge. In a paradise of natural abundance no economic theory would be required or become possible. Pecuniary value is the measure of scarcity in the provision of utility, but it is the "cost" of

[1] Assisted by the specious though erroneous application of Marginalism even so humane an economist as Philip Wicksteed committed himself to the view that the play of modern economic forces gave every man the "worth" of his work. "So far as the vigilance of communal instincts and motives can secure any end, we may assume that they are already getting as much as their work is worth, and that our problem is partly perhaps to see that they get (not from their employers and customers, but from communal funds) something more than they are worth, but very certainly to see whether they cannot be made worth more." (*The Common Sense of Political Economy*, 1st edition, p. 345.) Since there normally exists no "surplus" from which a communal fund may be drawn, and some expenditure on education and other services would be needed to make them "worth more," it is manifest that the rigorous logic of this Marginalism offers no solution of the human problem. A little reflection, however, enables us to recognize that the statement that every worker gets what he is "worth" means nothing more than that he gets what he can get—a not very illuminative proposition.

this provision, not the utility which is the matter of direct pecuniary account.

Valuation by relative costs would enable different classes of goods to be produced, exchanged, distributed and consumed, in accordance with minimum cost and maximum utility in a frictionless competitive system. The assumption that takes for granted the existence of such a system is the main "preconception" of the classical economics. The practical preoccupation of economists with measures, commercial and pecuniary, for removing the friction and the barriers that interfere with this basic assumption have given them an air of benefaction and of fair play which is absent from the actualities of the economic situation.

Veblen is quick to discern the radical defects of such a scientific approach. It assumes an economic world which neither exists nor can exist. It is false in its assumptions that economic activity is directed mainly or exclusively by "hedonist" aims, that individual gains add up to make social gains, and that "free" competition operates "normally" throughout the economic system, so as to distribute income in proportion to "costs," whether these costs be measured in pecuniary terms or in terms of personal sacrifice. Such plausibility as could be rendered to an economic science based on assumptions so contrary to the visible facts, can only be explained by the strange vogue among Victorian intellectuals of a belief that political and economic equality was advancing in ways which would rapidly remove the barriers between the social classes and the different nations so as to achieve that frictionless competition needed to realize their assumption. A democratic franchise, with equal access to education and knowledge from free teaching and a free Press, with the achievement of free trade, free movements for capital and labour throughout the world—these were demands which the "natural" tendencies and achievements of the new age of progress were destined to fulfil!

Were such an interpretation of the equilitarian movement valid, it would carry with it a warrant for the "taxonomic" attitude of classical economists towards an economic system based on a static equilibrism. This taxonomic attitude Veblen well summarizes in his remarks upon Marshall's work. "Any sympathetic reader of Professor Marshall's great work—comes away with a sense of swift and smooth movement and interaction of parts; but it is the movement of a consummately conceived and self-balanced mechanism, not that of a cumulatively unfolding process or an institutional adaptation to cumulatively unfolding exigencies."[1]

The laws of such a political economy are in a

[1] Op. cit., p. 173.

word "laws of conservation and selection, not of genesis and prolification."[1] He still finds a lack of the evolutionary treatment—of economic processes. Yet it is admitted that Marshall and the leading American economists had gone far from the conception of the economics of Mill and his school. In balancing cost and utility as expressed through supply and demand in the market, and in his humanistic interpretation of both terms Marshall had laid the foundation of a science which, as Veblen admits, had "an air of evolutionism."

I think it must be admitted that the disturbing hostile attitude of Veblen towards the neo-classical economics, based on his charge of "taxonomy" remains unconvincing to many of his readers, until they are brought into contact with his own positive interpretation of the economic system as he found it working in the America of his time.

Far more immediately convincing is his criticism of the "theorem of equivalence": "the postulate which lies at the root of the classical theory of distribution."[2] For this equivalence between the activities, or "costs," of the several factors of production and the product distributed among them as real income would appear to have the certitude attaching to the general scientific law of conservation of energy, as well as the equity attaching to the

[1] Op. cit., p. 177.   [2] Op. cit., p. 281.

PLACE OF ECONOMICS IN THE SCIENCES

postulate of natural rights. For what can be more reasonable and just than that the aggregate product of a joint productive effort shall be apportioned to the several factors according to their respective contributions?

It is to Veblen's challenge of the soundness of this doctrine of "equivalence" that we can best turn for an understanding of his position as a reconstructionist of economic theory.

For if the whole product is necessarily swallowed up in bare costs of production, no "surplus" can exist and no conflict can emerge for the possession of this surplus. Economic peace and order are secured with justice to all parties concerned: economic progress will consist in the higher productivity which the several forms of "cost" may yield, and the increasing product will be distributed in accordance with the greater productivity of the several factors in production. Though the logic of this process of apportioning the fruits of economic progress may seem dubious, the classical economists were upon the whole content to manipulate the cost theory of value so as to absorb the whole product in natural costs, leaving no surplus over for contention between the owners of the several factors of production. "Under the resulting natural-economic law of equivalence and equity, it is held that the several participants or factors in the economic process severally get the equivalent of the productive force which they expend. They severally get as much as they produce; and conversely in the normal case they severally produce as much as they get."[1]

Veblen's closest investigation of this natural equity of distribution under modern capitalism is found in his discussion of the writings of Professor J. B. Clark, a leading American economist of the last generation. Though Clark is distinguished from other economists in minor matters of theory, he is the plainest and best exponent of the hedonist competitive school in its application of the doctrine of "marginal utility" as the key to a natural and equitable distribution of the whole product. In a productive operation where capital and labour are engaged, each succeeding unit of capital and of labour is somewhat less productive than the preceding ones until you come to a unit which it is only just worth while to employ because its product only just covers its "remuneration." This statement, however, requires a qualification. For in most businesses the earlier additions of units of

[1] P. 284. Though rent was still treated as a sort of surplus, it had a "natural" origin in the productivity of the land, and since legal possession is the accepted basis of all "right" of property, the owner of the land receives rent as the share that belongs to him. The fact that rent was treated quite erroneously as consisting entirely of differential surplus measured from a no-rent margin, some landowners obtaining no rent, may have helped to give a sense of equity to the rent element in distribution.

capital and labour are often more productive than the first unit, so that up to a certain size each new unit appears to be more productive than the earlier ones. It is not until a law of diminishing returns begins to operate that the measure of marginal utility becomes operative. But in every form of business such a limit obtains, applicable to every separate factor of production. "The total product created by the labour so engaged is at the same time the distributive share received by such labour as wages, and it equals that increment of product added by the 'final' unit of labour, multiplied by the number of such units engaged. The law of 'natural' interest is the same as this law of wages, with a change of terms. The product of each unit of labour or capital being measured by the product of the 'final' unit, each gets the amount of its own product."[1] Curiously enough Veblen does not directly expose the fallacious assumption contained in this presentation, in that the total product will always exceed the product of the final unit multiplied by the number of units. This is evaded by marginalists who contend that since any one of the units may be taken as the marginal one, payment of wages or interest at the marginal rate of productivity is an equitable rate giving equal payment to each unit of capital and labour.

[1] Professor Clark's *Economics*, p. 202.

He attacks the hedonism of Clark on the ground that "there can be no balance and no commeasurability, between the laborer's disability (pain) in producing the goods and the consumer's utility (pleasure) in consuming them, insomuch as these two hedonistic phenomena lie each within the consciousness of a distinct person." Hence "the wages of labor (i.e. the utility of the goods received by the laborer) is not equal to the disability undergone by him, except in the sense that he is competitively willing to accept it; nor are these wages equal to the utility got by the consumer of the goods except in the sense that he is competitively willing to pay them."[1]

Veblen does not, however, here or elsewhere, adopt the theory of organic determination which denies any separate causative influence to a final unit, either in a system of production or a system (standard) of consumption. The final or marginal theory is wrecked upon the simple fact that in an organic system no separate cost or utility can rightly be accorded to any constituent unit of that system. Neither in theory nor in practice does the planner of a business assign a separate cost or productivity to any final unit of the capital or labour he proposes to employ. It is quite true that he considers closely how many machines he shall put in and how many workers of different grades he

[1] Op. cit., p. 204.

shall employ. But he recognizes clearly that in this estimate no separate utility can be attributed to a single machine or a single worker. Similarly with the standard of consumption and the family outlay, the notion of the marketing mistress consciously balancing the exact utility of each shilling spent on a number of separate articles of produce, so that the money spent on the last egg shall yield the same utility or satisfaction as the last pair of stockings, is entirely false to the facts of the economic process. Margins can be discovered by analyses, and the consequent assumption may be sound that marginal purchases can be deemed to give equal utilities. But these margins are not the conscious causes or determinants of the outlay, but are its implications or results. The planner of a business does, of course, estimate as closely as he can the numbers of the different machines he shall put in, the size of the different departments, the quantity of power he shall require and the number of machine-tenders, foremen, clerks and other employees. But he does not assign a separate value to each of these units of capital and labour; he regards them as co-operative factors in a composite organic structure. Similarly with the outlay of the family income, each item is regarded not as yielding a separate utility but as a composite element in a standard of living.

There are passages in Veblen where he approaches this criticism of marginalism, but he is mainly concerned with a repudiation of the hedonist calculus it employs.[1]

[1] The repudiation of hedonism enters so deeply into Veblen's quarrel with the Classical Economics that it is necessary here to explain the importance he attached to it. Even when the preconception of natural law, in the sense of an overruling Providence, or "an invisible hand" had passed into the background of economic exposition, the sense of a normal economic behaviour of men and occurrences which gave "a body of maxims for the conduct of business" that worked out for the material gain of all concerned, underlay the theory of economics. In the detailed activities of man along this line of advantageous normality, his desire for some pleasurable end is his direct determinant. All man's productive activities are directed by this conscious motive. This explains the willingness to undergo tedious and irksome toil or to postpone immediate in favour of future expenditure and enjoyment. "Hedonistic exchange value is the outcome of a valuation process enforced by the apprehended pleasure-giving capacity of the items valued." (Quoted Dorfman, p. 157.)

The underlying assumption of this Hedonism is that pleasure consciously and directly determines what a man shall do, whereas in fact his aptitudes determine what is pleasurable to him. Wages and activities precede, pleasures follow. "In Hedonistic theory the substantive end of economic life is individual gain and the utilitarian philosophy makes the sum of the gains of individuals the gain of society, so that an individual in serving his own interests in acquisition serves the interests of society to the extent that he is successful." (Dorfman, p. 157). Elsewhere the same criticism is expressed by Veblen in an article in the *Journal of Political Economy*, thus: "Pleasure (or desire for pleasure) is not itself a primary factor of consciousness. . . . Pleasure is the feeling concomitant of certain states or modes of activity. . . . Pleasure, in other words, results from the attainment of some already existent end of action; it is not in itself an end." (Dorfman, p. 157.)

To many psychologists and sociologists Veblen will appear to drive to an extreme his anti-hedonism, when he makes it a ground for repudiating the whole utilitarian calculus or method of valuation. For the most primitive urges to activity in a human being, or any animal, cannot be explained except as desired escapes from some static condition, some action conducive to personal safety. Nor can it be denied that such activities, once established as methods of escape, begin to carry elements of conscious satisfaction in their performance. Such biological utility is always touched with conscious satisfaction, and the practice of the activity carries an immediate pleasure. The denial of such conscious satisfaction as a motive must lead to a doctrine of "behaviourism," which is not really held by Veblen, and which his economic determinism does not require.

"The hedonistically presumed final purchases of consumable goods are not habitually contemplated in the pursuit of business enterprise. Business men habitually aspire to accumulate wealth in excess of the limits of practicable consumption, and the wealth so accumulated is not intended to be converted by a final transaction of purchase into consumable goods or sensations of consumption. Such commonplace facts as these, together with the endless web of business detail of a like pecuniary character, do not in hedonistic theory raise a question as to how those conventional aims, ideals, aspirations and standards have come into force, or how they affect the scheme of life in business or outside of it; they do not raise these questions because such questions cannot be answered in the terms which the hedonistic economists are content to use, or, indeed, what their premises permit them to use."[1]

One other issue of high importance arises in considering the final or marginal determination of prices. Such determination carries with it a rejection of any equitable distribution through the price system. "Price is determined, competitively, by marginal producers or sellers and marginal consumers or purchasers: the latter alone, on the one side, get the precise price-equivalent of the

[1] Op. cit., p. 249.

disability incurred by them, and the latter alone, on the other side, pay the full price-equivalent of the utilities desired by them from the goods purchased."[1]

Thus on each side of the bargain relation there remains an uncovered "surplus" for the apportionment of which no reasonable or equitable law is provided. This irrational surplus emerges in all markets save in the ideal case where it is equally important for all sellers to sell and for all buyers to buy and where there exists perfectly free competition in the economic system. But marginalists cannot maintain that in modern business either of these conditions actually operates. In an increasing number of industries an element of natural or planned monopoly prevents by restriction of output the formation of a genuinely competitive price, while in those markets where competition still exists there is a wide difference between the bargaining powers and gains of the different non-marginal sellers and buyers.

Thus under the classical economics, as fortified by the marginalist doctrine, no rational account of distribution can emerge. A reasonable, natural and equitable distribution is simply "assumed."

[1] Op. cit., p. 208.

CHAPTER III

VEBLEN'S ATTITUDE TOWARDS MARX

THESE diverse and often difficult criticisms of current economic theory may serve to introduce us to the central positive structure of Veblen's economic thesis, viz., the contrast and opposition between industrial and pecuniary employments. But before opening out upon this topic it may be well to set forth briefly Veblen's attitude towards Socialism and in particular the Marxist form of Socialism.

Veblen deals with this topic in a general essay on *The Theory of Socialism* and in published lectures on *The Economics of Karl Marx* delivered at Harvard University in 1906, and republished in *The Place of Science in Modern Civilization*. His general treatment is directed to the analysis of the complex of emotional and intellectual motives that inspire the socialist movement, especially in its American setting.

The chief source of unrest and of dissatisfaction with the economic system in America, as Veblen saw it, was not so much its waste or its injustice, or the poverty it imposes on the workers, as the growing difficulty it presents to the achievement of the human sense of dignity, which attaches to economic success. "In our fundamentally industrial society a person should be economically successful if he would enjoy the esteem of his fellow men."[1] For such success implies "worth" with some flavour of a moral implication attaching to the business efficiency of the man. It makes him socially respectable. But respectability, in the sense of conformity to an accepted standard, is not enough. The competitive factor of emulation, the desire to make a better show than your neighbour, has played a part of increasing importance in modern America. In every modern industrial country the possession and display of wealth have been a growing agent in determining social status. But in most other countries birth, class and other traditional barriers have stood in the way of the social climber. In America such barriers, though existent in some Eastern centres, have been relatively feeble. Economic success has been more rapid, more frequent, and more sensational in its magnitude than elsewhere. Veblen thus summarizes the situation in its broad general aspect. "The outcome of modern industrial development has been—to intensify emulation and the jealousy

[1] *The Place of Science*, p. 393.

that goes with emulation, and to focus the emulation and the jealousy on the possession and enjoyment of material goods."[1] Now so long as every energetic pushful man thinks he has a fair chance of obtaining economic success by adhering to the rules of the existing business game he is unlikely to quarrel with the current economic order. But when that economic order itself closes the avenues of opportunity to the acquisition of wealth, and the control of business is visibly passing into the hands of an industrial and financial oligarchy, discontent and a widespread restlessness begin to rouse criticism of that order and control. Though this state of mind does not normally imply hostility to the institution of private property or a demand for socialization, it evidently calls for some radical changes in the current arrangements. Had Veblen survived to see the boiling up of the passions aroused by the collapse of the post-War era of prosperity and the widespread dismay at the long-continued depression, his judgment, expressed so far back as 1892,[2] regarding the sources and motives of the then latent or inchoate "socialism" of the American people would have been strongly confirmed. While most politicians and economists of the last generation saw no signs of that early

[1] Op. cit., p. 397.
[2] "Some neglected points in the Theory of Socialism" (*Annals of the American Academy of Political and Social Science*, Vol. II).

development of governmental processes which is so conspicuous everywhere to-day, Veblen's acute reading of certain signs of the time is disclosed in the following observation. "The right of eminent domain and the power to tax, as interpreted under modern constitutional forms, indicate something of the direction of development of the political functions of society at a point where they touch the province of the industrial system. It is along the line indicated by these and other kindred facts that the socialists are advancing."[1] Though the rapid progress made along these lines of fragmentary State socialism within recent years in every "capitalist" country since the Great War could not then have been predicted, the present spasmodic plunges into taxation for business aids and social services, accompanied by experiments in compulsory centralization, price- and wage-fixing with demands for wealth-sharing by heavier direct taxes and by "public subsidies," well illustrate the sort of socialism in America the beginnings of which Veblen detected early in the 'nineties.

Neither then nor now was Marxist socialism a strong trend in the process of American discontent. This is attributable partly to the fact that the Marxist propaganda came through the utterances of foreign immigrants of recent date and was dis-

[1] Op. cit., p. 404.

counted by "good Americans." But a more potent reason lay in the intellectual and moral dislike of general formulas and forcible revolutions for their wholesale adoption in a country where no widespread belief in the necessity or desirability of revolutionary methods existed. Nor can it be said that the Marxian theories commended themselves to any school of American economic thinkers, or that their chief reason for rejecting those theories lay in their interested attachment to the capitalist system. Even if most American economists might be expected to show an interested reluctance to adopt Marxism, this would certainly not apply to Veblen. Therefore his attitude towards Marxism rightly deserves a close consideration. Now this is not an easy task. For the plain thinker Marxism is obscured at the outset by the Hegelism dialectic applied to a materialistic conception of history which is the very reverse of the spiritual process which Hegel himself applies. The struggle to which Hegel applies his three-phase dialectic (thesis, antithesis, synthesis) is a struggle of the spirit towards a fuller self-realization. In the Marxist system the struggle becomes a class struggle for material wealth. But as Veblen points out, material is not the right word to describe the actual process even in the Marxist theory. For the class struggle is not material in the sense of physical or even physiological. It is economic, but the motive forces lie in "the spiritual plane of human desire and passion." "It is a sublimated materialism, sublimated by the dominating presence of the conscious human spirit; but it is conditioned by the material facts of the production of the means of life."[1]

Economic production thus envisaged by Marx is the output or material expression of the life-process as applied in an expenditure of labour-power. This expended labour-power produces more than the cost required to sustain it, and this increase of product constitutes a surplus-value which under the capitalist system goes in profit to the owners of capital. Capitalism thus presented is a matter of competitive profit-making. If the labourer took the full product of his labour, the real value of his product would correspond with its exchange value, and no surplus element would emerge. It is one of the obscurities of the Marxian reasoning that Marx appears to hold that, even where there exists free competition among capitalists, this surplus element is held as profit. He seems to think it enough to show that labour produces more than its cost, or "keep" and that this excess passes into the employer's hands. If, however, free competition

[1] Op. cit., p. 415.

VEBLEN'S ATTITUDE TOWARDS MARX

in marketing the product occurred, it might reasonably be held that capitalists must by the natural operation of the price system hand over to working-class consumers the bulk of the surplus, only retaining what corresponds to the minimum payment needed to evoke their saving and capital-creation.

Marxism, however, is committed to the accumulation of capital by a continuous process, accurately summarized by Veblen in the following terms: "Wages being the (approximately exact) value of labor-power bought in the wages contract; the price of the product being the (similarly approximate) value of the goods produced; and since the value of the product exceeds that of the labor-power by a given amount (surplus value) which by force of the wage-contract passes into the possession of the capitalist and is by him in part laid by as savings and added to the capital already in hand, it follows (α) that, other things equal, the larger the surplus value, the more rapid the increase of capital; and also (β) that, the greater the increase of capital relatively to the labor-force employed, the more productive the labor employed and the larger the surplus product available for accumulation. The process of accumulation, therefore, is evidently a cumulative one; and, also evidently, the increase added to capital is an unearned increment drawn from the unpaid surplus product of labor."[1]

Veblen points out that this process might reasonably be held to lead to a growing inability of the rate of consumption to keep pace with the growth of production due to this accumulation of capital, and that such a maladjustment between production and markets would lead to the breakdown of the capitalist system "and so by its own force will bring on the socialist consummation."[2]

Marx, however, was so strongly committed to the conscious class-struggle operative through a proletarian revolution, that such a natural transformation could not be entertained by him. It is deeply significant that to-day socialism in many countries, especially in Britain and America, is divided into two schools, the revolutionists who adhere to the notion that capitalism can only yield to the force of a conscious proletarian revolution, and the gradualists who, moving along the lines of the nationalization of key industries, together with highly graduated taxation for improved social services, and with a higher wages and larger leisure programme, would expedite the natural downfall of capitalism due to a failure to obtain profitable markets for its potential product.

Veblen, however, is most deeply concerned with

[1] Op. cit., p. 425.   [2] Op. cit., p. 426.

tracing the effects which the Darwinian conception of evolution exercised upon the original Marxism. The class-struggle, as conceived by Marx, was based upon a rational calculus of material gains operating persistently towards a socialistic goal. But "Under the Darwinian norm it must be held that man's reasoning is largely controlled by other than logical, intellectual forces; that the conclusion reached by public or class opinion is as much, or more, a matter of sentiment than of logical inference; and that the sentiment which animates men, singly or collectively, is as much, or more, an outcome of habit and native propensity as of calculated material interest. There is, for instance, no warrant in the Darwinian scheme of things, for asserting *a priori* that the class-interest of the working class will bring them to make a stand against the propertied class"—"It may be that the working classes will go forward along the line of the socialistic ideals and enforce a new deal in which there shall be no economic class discrepancies, no intentional animosity, no dynastic politics. But then it may also, so far as can be foreseen, equally well happen that the working class, with the rest of the community in Germany, England or America, may be led by the habit of loyalty and by their sportsmanlike propensities to lend themselves enthusiastically to the game of dynastic politics which alone their sportsmanlike rulers consider worth while."[1]

The influence of Darwinism superimposed on the early Marxism is to substitute for the narrower conception of an economic drive conducted along logical lines of conscious gain, the broader conception of the communal concern with a mixed output of instinctive urges of which reason is more the servant than the master.[2]

The Darwinian influence not only substitutes a larger variety of animal urges for the single economic drive to social conduct. It gets rid of the belief in a final socialistic achievement. There is no goal in the evolutionary process, as Veblen sees it. "It is a scheme of blindly cumulative causation, in which there is no trend, no fixed term, no consummation. The sequence is controlled by nothing but the *vis a tergo* of brute causation and is essentially mechanical."[3]

Fully assimilated, this hard Darwinianism would seem to destroy the main doctrines of Marxism.

---

[1] When it is borne in mind that these lectures were delivered in 1906, the interpretative genius of Veblen will be realized.

[2] "The weakness of Marx was that he emphasized inner necessity, self-interest, as factors in the change to socialism, rather than the influence of environment. The defect is being remedied by the modern socialists bringing in the Darwinian principle that the selective principle of survival is adaptation to a changing environment which human activity has itself created, and that unless such adaptation takes place the organism must perish." (Dorfman p. 244.)

[3] Op. cit., p. 436.

VEBLEN'S ATTITUDE TOWARDS MARX

The class-war with its revolutionary ending, as the revolt against the increasing misery of the workers due to the absorption of an ever-larger portion of the product of labour by a capitalist class of exploiters, could find no support from the Darwinian teaching. Considerable departures from the rigid Marxian teaching have been made in the ranks of Marx's followers in Germany and elsewhere so as to bring the socialist policy into closer conformity with recent scientific teaching in the fields of biology and psychology. Indeed, one or two of the basic conceptions of Marx are found incompatible with the facts of recent history, notoriously his doctrine of the "increasing misery" of the wage-earners. Most modern socialists recognize that some considerable improvement has been taking place in the conditions of labour in most countries, and they rely upon this improvement not as a damage but as an aid to the socialist movement. For well-conditioned workers will fight more effectively for the maintenance and improvement of their standard of life than "an anæmic working class under the pressure of abject privation."

Again, the early attitude adopted by Marxists towards the Trade Unions movement is seen no longer to be tenable. For Trade Unionism has been found also to strengthen the position of the workers in demanding higher wages and other improved conditions. The newer attitude even among avowed Marxists has been that it is desirable to permeate Trade Unions, and to bring their narrower industrial aims into conformity with the broader socialist policy.

Two other important modifications are noted by Veblen. One is the attitude towards agriculture. Though a rigorous communism might strive, as in the early years of Soviet Russia, to impose a thorough socialism upon the peasant class, it is now usually recognized that this is a wasteful and impracticable policy, and that a wider meaning must be given to the sense of private property among cultivators of the soil than is recognized in ordinary industry. Though Veblen was writing long before the Great War and the Russian revolution, his understanding of the American Middle-West enabled him to perceive the fatuity of any endeavour to foist a full socialism upon the farmer. He foresaw those demands of the peasant-farmer for reasonable prices and markets, and for relief from the exactions of creditors, which stand out so clearly to-day in the disturbed American situation. The other modification of socialism concerns its political aspect. Veblen perceives the growing permeation of social democracy by the views of national jingoism. "The Spokesmen now are concerned to show that, while they stand for international socialism, consonant with their ancient position, they stand for national aggrandisement first, and for international comity second."[1] Such criticism, delivered in 1906, wears the cloak of genuine scientific prophecy.

Most of those who reject the Marxist teaching and the policies it is designed to promote betray in their writings an animus which rightly impairs their influence upon the minds of truth-seekers. But though Veblen rejects most of the Marxist doctrines, he is singularly free from emotional bias in doing so. He evidently regards Marx as a great original thinker, and accepts for himself as a substantial basic truth the economic determinism which Marx adopts, though he applies it differently. Indeed, the application of economic determinism in a novel form to the human conduct of men in his own country, as the typical capitalist country, may be regarded as the essential contribution Veblen makes to the thought of his time.

[1] Op. cit., p. 454.

CHAPTER IV

VEBLEN'S SOCIALISM

VEBLEN'S criticism of Marx's economics by stressing their differences has perhaps tended to conceal their resemblances. Both are economic determinists in the sense that they regard economic activities, conditions and aims, as the main factors in forming other social institutions for the pursuit of personal and social ends that lie outside the directly economic sphere. Both would agree that the nature of man contains other urges, tendencies, proclivities and interests, which, in varying degrees and in differing environments, exercise an independent influence upon man's economic life—thus qualifying the principle of economic determination of history. Both hold the doctrine of conflict of interests between an owning class and a producing class. But their conception of this conflict is different. Marxist socialism sees the capitalist employer taking in profits the product created by the workers he employs, in excess of that portion essential to maintain them in the necessary physical efficiency and to reproduce themselves. Veblen, though holding that the producers are exploited by owners, takes a different view of the processes of production and of the modern technique of exploitation. The productivity of workers on the soil or in the factory depends for its amount and quality not entirely and not chiefly upon their working energy, but upon economic conditions under which they work that lie outside their personal control. First and foremost among these conditions is the state of the industrial arts, a rich social inheritance of long accumulation, which is the basis of all skilled workmanship. No living worker or group of workers can properly lay claim to this accumulated knowledge as his private possession, though he is entitled to utilize it in order to increase his productivity. Again, the size of the population in any economic group and the civilized needs which seek satisfaction through exchange of economic goods and services are social conditions that affect the individual worker's productivity. For the demand, which comes from acquired and transmitted habits and standards of consumption, continually growing and changing in every civilized community, reacts upon the character and productivity of all the arts of production.

These arts of production and consumption, however, imply the existence of and access to the natural resources of the earth—the material basis of all economic processes. These natural resources may on any equitable consideration be regarded as the social inheritance of each succeeding generation of man with equal rights of utilization.

"The Great Adventure of the Americans has, after all, been the seizure of the fertile land and its conversion to private gain. Their dealing with the soil has been the largest of those enterprises in absentee ownership, both in respect of its extent in time and space and in its social and civil consequences."[1]

These distinctively social sources of wealth must be taken as important qualifications of the cruder socialism in which the worker is held to create all wealth and the capitalist employer to take all "the surplus." But they do not, of course, impair the essential truth of the exploitation of labour. In modern civilized countries these social sources have passed into the legal possession and the economic control of the owner of capital and the organizers of industry, and the rent and profit they yield are large factors in the accumulation of unearned wealth. But their main use is realized in the superior bargaining power they afford to employers in dealing with labour.

So far, however, we have not touched the salient fact of the origin, ownership and use of capital, in its practical meaning of the tools,

[1] *Absentee Ownership*, p. 169.

machinery, surplus food, raw materials and power held and utilized for employing labour in turning out goods to be sold for profit. The modern supply of these concrete forms of capital takes place chiefly through the pecuniary process of investment. These capital-goods, Veblen holds, with Marx, are products of labour and the interest they earn for their possessors is due to the fact that their producers are paid for producing them less than their worth when used as instruments of production in accordance with the technological knowledge at the service of the community. Veblen does not discuss in this connexion the first origins of capital, as representing the tools, or the extra supplies of food or materials, due to the longer day's work of men working on their own account and willing to put in some extra work after satisfying their immediate needs. The concrete capital with which he is concerned is the existing tools, machines, materials and power, created by the labour of workmen, who are furnished with wages that give them their necessary food and other supports of the working life. The pecuniary capital consists of money derived from the ownership of land or capital goods, or from the high remuneration paid to members of the lucrative professions. Such surplus income could, of course, have been spent upon luxuries or other consumption goods, but by the process of investment it has been spent in the purchase of capital goods which earn interest for the owners. Thus envisaged, investment yields no productive utility and involves no personal cost on the part of the investor. It is simply a method of "getting something for nothing"—to use a familiar phrase in Veblen's writings, employed to designate all predatory processes. If a Crusoe economy or even a communist economy were the subject of analysis, it would have been impossible to deny that the extra labour involved in adding to the stock of capital goods, or, put otherwise, in postponing present consumption or leisure in favour of a larger quantity of future consumption or leisure, constituted a "cost" and furnished a utility.

Even taking our modern economic system as it is, it is difficult to understand how Veblen could so completely detach the pecuniary aspect of investment from the concrete goods it brought into existence through stimulating an increased demand for capital goods. It must, however, be remembered that the "cost" or sacrifice of saving, though very real for the worker or the small farmer, amounts to very little among the wealthier classes who "save" and "invest" only the surplus that remains after their customary comforts and luxuries are purchased. Moreover, the increasing proportion of savings which take the form of profits put into company reserves serves to mask the real nature of the saving process. So far as investment appears as an application to industry of surplus or unearned income it comes under the "predatory" category.

But the investment capital processes which occupied Veblen's attention lay outside the recognized methods of accepted economic theory. It is in the capitalization of "intangible assets" that Veblen finds the key-stone of the pecuniary dominion exercised by modern financiers. More and more in modern America he sees the ownership and control of big industry passing from the ordinary shareholder and the employer to groups of financiers who have no direct contact with industry, but are purely concerned with manipulation of pecuniary capital. In dealing with real estate the contemplated future values of land and its accessories in a growing community are made the subjects of speculative finance, by means of which large profits may accrue to this type of banker or other financier. But the biggest financial exploits are concerned with amalgamations and recapitalization of the stock and share values in the key industries. Whether it be trusts or looser forms of combination, or the development of holding companies, the technique of the pecuniary management of "intangible" assets, swelled by credit operations, signifies that the actual control of the key industries has passed more and more away from the industrial managers and the technical experts into the hands of men concerned solely to operate those industries in the interest of profits on inflated values and manipulations of the money market. This process of pecuniary control by amalgamation came into prominence in the late 'nineties in America, with the formation of the Standard Oil Trust, the United Steel Corporation and other more or less successful experiments in controlling other key industries. The distinction drawn by Veblen between the key industries, the minor manufactures, and agriculture, in respect of financial control, is of great importance to the comprehension of his economics.

Steel, Oil, Coal and Railways had been getting into a dangerous condition of cut-throat competition by the early 'nineties. Rapid changes of industrial processes and the appropriation of new material resources had put many of the older business concerns out of date and their competitive market became more and more precarious by reason of the increasing volume of productive power and the limitation of the profitable home market even under the shelter of a high protective tariff. Many of these businesses got into financial difficulties and their own financial skill and means were quite unequal to coping with the situation. It was then that the great opportunity for the investment banker arose. Veblen thus describes his *modus operandi*. "The holding-company and the mergers, together with the interlocking directorates, and presumably the voting trust, were the ways and means by which the banking community took over the strategic regulation of the key industries, and by way of that avenue also the control of the industrial system at large. By this move the effectual direction in all that concerns the business management of the key industries was taken out of the hands of corporation managers working in severalty and at cross purposes, and has been lodged in the hands of that group of investment bankers who constitute in effect a General Staff of financial strategy, and who between them command the general body of the credit resources."[1]

It was under the pressure and by the active aid of these financial groups that the consolidation of the steel interests was achieved at a cost of "a bonus in the form of a block of the new corporation's securities bearing a face value of $50,000,000 in which sum the new corporation formally became indebted to its sponsors, as payment for their services. This bonus was in the nature of an addition to the corporation's capitalization. And it may be

[1] *Absentee Ownership*, p. 339.

added that in the end, after some further financial manœuvres, the securities which made up this bonus came to be worth fully their face value."[1]

It might seem that this final sentence was an economic justification of the policy and that it indicated a scrapping of obsolete methods, a better technical organization of the hitherto wastefully competing plants and various economies of salesmanship. In other words, it might be justified as the creation of new real values. But this is not the way it presents itself to Veblen. He sees in it a creation of "intangible assets" by an increased extension of credit, operated so as to give a higher pecuniary value to the same body of concrete business capital. These intangible assets "are wholly in the nature of an absentee claim to a share in the country's income; in the last analysis, of course, a claim upon the product of industry, to which all the while they have contributed nothing."[2]

But, it may be objected, if several groups of financiers are engaged in this amalgamation and credit-expanding process, will they not cut one another's throats? To this Veblen replies that "In effect, whether it runs to commercial banking or in the field of investment, banking is essentially not now a competitive business, except collectively as against the underlying population. And invest-

[1] Op. cit., p. 344.   [2] Op. cit., p. 347 note.

ment banking in an eminent degree is a line of enterprise in which it is incumbent upon all the parties in interest to take hands and help, in which one good turn deserves another, and in which there can be no tolerance for men who wantonly disregard the rules of the game."[1]

This analysis makes evident the opposition between the industrialist, whose primary concern is to operate the plant and labour at his disposal so as to obtain the maximum output of goods, and the financier who is concerned only with the profits which industry can be made to yield. This opposition is conceived by Veblen as unqualified by any consideration of the higher specialization of technique rendered possible by amalgamations and by the reduced waste of competitive marketing. These advantages he does not apparently regard as economic utilities. Indeed the whole art of salesmanship is represented as an operation in human credulity, whether the method used be public advertising or personal solicitation. The advancing sales-cost of so many articles in common use he attributes largely to the fact that their reduced production cost by modern technique can be and is absorbed in increased sales costs. This last consideration must apply not to the key products which have yielded to the process of amalgamation

[1] Op. cit., p. 350.

but to the ordinary final products where excessive production is still attended by keen competition. Indeed one of the chief diseases of our modern economic system is the immense increase of futile energy represented by the growing personnel of those engaged in advertising and in wholesale and retail selling.

This, however, is not the main charge Veblen makes against finance control of industry. That charge is one of "sabotage," by which he means the deliberate policy of curtailing or restricting production in order to obtain a larger volume of profit out of selling a smaller product at a higher price. An absolute monopoly with power to dictate monopoly prices is, no doubt, a comparatively rare thing. For few monopolies are absolute in their exclusive ownership of a supply, and few articles are so indispensable as to admit of no substitutes. But with these provisos in mind, we must admit that the processes of financial control described by Veblen do lend themselves to the two related abuses of monopoly, restriction of productive energy, and dictated prices higher than would prevail in a free market.

Now such a financial policy is injurious to the under classes alike in their capacity of worker and consumer. By restricting production it holds a permanent surplus of unemployed labour to be kept alive at the expense of other workers or out of public funds. This unemployed surplus prevents an effective organization of labour, thus enabling employers to keep down wages and in some instances to practise a sweating system as regards both pay and hours. By the higher prices of final goods the real wages of the workers also suffer injury, for they form the bulk of the consumers of most staple commodities which fall under the restrictive policy.

The degree to which the finance power will practise this restriction of output and rise of prices will, of course, vary greatly in different industries. Where increasing output is attended by decreasing costs, it may be more profitable to put productive capital and labour to full use, provided that the price at which the larger output can be sold does not fall so much as to exceed the lower costs. This is a matter of the "elasticity of demand" and will vary with the nature of the goods, and the probability of the entry of new competing supplies in case the margin of profit is kept too high. But though it cannot therefore be held that a policy of financial sabotage will always be found profitable, the assumption that an outside financial control will interfere with the disposition of the industrialist to put his capital and labour to its full use is generally valid for the key industries and for many if not most of the industries dependent on them for some important materials.

Veblen was writing before the recent general collapse of industry in America, which he would have regarded as a striking endorsement of his analysis. It is true that its first phase, the collapse of credits and the failure of the majority of country banks (with not a few great city banks) might appear at first sight to contravene his general thesis of a credit system sucking the profits out of industry. For on the surface it was the credit-giving banks whose failure precipitated the industrial and agricultural collapse with its attendant unemployment and distress. But this surface view ignores the salient fact that, owing, partly, to rapid recent technological improvements, especially in key industries, and, partly, to the cessation of those post-War foreign loans which took off large surpluses of American foodstuffs, raw materials and manufactured goods, the excessive pace of American production as compared with consumption suddenly developed at a pace that brought a fall of prices which destroyed everywhere industrial confidence, and brought a voluntary sabotage of production. This situation preceded the great financial crash which then reacted upon most branches of industry, agriculture and commerce, extending the waste of capital and labour and blocking the road to recovery.

VEBLEN'S SOCIALISM

It may, however, be doubted whether Veblen's logical account of the periodic practice of industrial sabotage by the overruling financial owners completely fits the recent situation. For though the collapse of the weaker financial institutions may be represented as contributory to the closer control of the big financial survivors, there are signs that the money power recognizes some limits to its credit profiteering policy imposed by the insufficiency of consuming power in the hands of the under-classes. Though Veblen sometimes approached this consideration, he did not give it the value which Marx attached to it, as threatening a necessary collapse of capitalism. Towards the end of his work on *Absentee Ownership*, however, we find a passage or two where he prophesies a general decay of the productive arts as the result of financial strangling. "At every move the interest of technological inter-relations will be drawn to a finer mesh, a more close-knit and more widely inclusive web of give and take, within which the working balance of co-ordination runs on a continually closer margin of tolerance. With the result that a disturbance, in the nature of retardation or deficiency at any critical point, will carry derangement and sabotage further and faster than before through the main lines and into the intricate working details of production. With every further move along the lines on which the industrial arts are advancing, therefore, sabotage—that is to say strategic unemployment at the instance of the owner-employers or of the workmen—becomes a swifter and more widely corrosive agency of miscarriage and decay."[1]

"In the long run," he holds, people will come to recognize that "something must be done about it." But the remedial measures they are likely to try will be of "a business-like nature"—"designed in all reason to safeguard the accomplished facts of absentee ownership in the natural resources involved and in the capitalized overhead charges which have been incorporated in the business. Necessarily so, for the community at large is addicted to business principles, and the official personnel is so addicted in an especial degree, in the nature of things."[2]

He admits, however, that "some sizeable element of the underlying population, not intrinsically committed to absentee ownership, will forsake or forget their moral principles of business-as-usual and will thereupon endeavour to take this business-like arrangement to pieces and put the works together again on some other plan, for better or for worse."[3]

This vague pronouncement is as near as he gets towards any prophecy of revolutionary reconstruc-

[1] *Absentee Ownership*, p. 421.   [2] Op. cit., p. 425.   [3] Op. cit., p. 425.

tion, to remedy the wilful sabotage of industry by finance. This vagueness is due neither to intellectual caution nor to lack of moral courage. He is not a revolutionist because he finds no adequate grounds for predicting what kind of direction the plunge of an exasperated people in America would be likely to take, or what results it would achieve.

For he is constantly aware of the strong sanctions which support every legalized form of ownership. The canons of respectability in profiteering are so powerfully implanted in the young of all classes in America by the schools, the Churches and the private opinion of all good citizens, that any effective action which can be stigmatized as radical, socialistic, or Bolshevik, still seems impossible to contemplate.

So powerfully is he impressed by the hold which money has acquired, not only over the operation of the economic processes but over the mental concepts of the business mind, that he seems to think that any deficiency in the physical output of goods brought about by financial sabotage will cause little trouble so long as the money-values are maintained. For, as he contends, "Money-values are the conclusive realities of business and the outstanding money-values will not suffer so long as the price per unit is suitably enhanced by a limitation of the output and an enlargement of the outstanding volume of purchasing power."[1] For the superstitious importance attached to money is by no means confined to the classes of those engaged in the financial and salesmanship processes. It so permeates the common mind that most workers would prefer a rise of their money wages even if they know that such a rise would be attended by a more than corresponding rise in the prices they paid for their consumption goods.

Though money for ordinary persons is admittedly a means and not an end, it has come for quite intelligible reasons to acquire a value on its own account, so that the perils and wrongs of inflation whether by governments or by private financiers evoke little reprobation unless they are of such dimensions as to cause immediate damage to livelihood by sudden rises of the price of the necessaries of life, or by sudden cancelment of savings—such as occurred in Germany in 1920.

The fact that in America speculation and gambling in credit values through the stock and share market have been so widespread among all classes (except the lower grades of wage-earners), has served to fasten upon the mind of ordinary men and women the belief that all gains got out of such practices are legitimate and even prestigious. This belief could not fail to throw a protective cloak

[1] Op. cit., p. 424.

over the larger and more consciously predatory practices of the professional financiers which Veblen endeavours to expose, and makes it difficult to believe that such an exposure will bring an early successful revolt against the domination of finance. Still less is such action likely to succeed in Britain and other European countries where the same sort of financial control over industry prevails, but where it is less audacious in its methods and where the arts of business combination are less mature.

In every advanced economic country the modern predatory practices receive support from the legal, political and moral traditions of an earlier and largely obsolescent structure of society. Nowhere is this more apparent than in America. This seems at first sight strange, almost paradoxical. For whereas in the older European communities law, constitution, business conditions and their prestigious supports, are derived from a long continuity of history which might be expected to cramp the adaptiveness of such societies to the moral requirements of a rapidly changing world, it might be expected that America, whose politics are derived from revolutionary changes of a century and a half ago, whose economic developments have been so swift and fearless, and where many immigrant peoples have contributed to the fluid mental outlook of the nation, would show a capacity of adaptation to the modern demands of the new technological and business methods with which no other nation could compete. But recent events shed an interesting light upon the political conservatism and the individualistic economics which still present formidable opposition to all attempts to apply remedies sufficiently drastic to deal with the wasting sickness of the time. The American Constitution obtained its compact construction at a time when revolutionary methods were not accompanied by any conception of evolution in politics. Put upon a reasonable and an equitable basis once for all, American life and the arrangements for carrying it on could properly be left to the freedom and the common sense of individual citizens seeking their own interests and freely co-operating for the attainment of their several group purposes. The material and human development of a great continent with limitless resources evoked a spirit of personal adventure and of the free exploitation of opportunities. Both the early colonial settlers and the subsequent flood of immigrants from various European countries were subject to informal processes of selection which yielded abnormal proportions of hardy, adventurous and self-assertive stock, men and women restless under home conditions, rebels against religious, political, industrial and social barriers, eager to work out their own salvation both in this world and the next. This belief in America as the land of free and equal opportunity, was a religion easily linked up with the sanctity of the Constitution and of the laws of property which secured for every man the share of land and other economic resources which his energy and adventure enabled him to take. Even when the era of rapid personal achievement ended with the close of the primary epoch and the emergence of great industrial mass-production under a few powerful groups, the tradition of the earlier times still kept its hold upon the popular mind and acquired a superstitious value. Thus it came to pass that the very absence of the competing superstitions of rank and caste which are still active in most European countries served to give added force to the prestige of economic achievement as attested by the growth of personal wealth, and to discount all criticism of the means by which such wealth had been acquired. Money became the sole criterion of personal success, and so long as the methods of its attainment did not contravene the laws, as interpreted by courts in sympathy with the moneyed class,[1]

[1] The corporation lawyer plays an important part in this economy. "He may fairly be called the legal strategist of high finance, the annex of the millionaire class. His business is corporate reorganization, the legal handling of the issues of taxation, the manipulation of receiverships, the penetration, on behalf of his clients, of those bulwarks erected by legislation to safeguard the public from the depredations of high finance." (H. J. Laski, "The Decline of the Professions," *Harper's Magazine*, November, 1935.)

public opinion not merely assented but applauded this order of prestigious achievement. It is not true that Americans love money for its own sake more than other people, but in America money has been the instrument by which personal power and prestige are attainable, to an extent that is not true of older countries. The financial exploitation which Veblen regards as the supreme achievement in America has, therefore, been assisted by the positive factor of economic enterprise in a country of rapidly developed resources, and by the negative factor of the absence of other competing sources of social prestige which are still found in older countries.[1]

[1] The following gradation of employments serves to illustrate Veblen's view. "Employments fall into a hierarchical gradation of respectability. Those which have to do immediately with ownership on a large scale are the most reputable of economic employments proper. Next to these in good repute come those employments that are immediately subservient to ownership and financieringc—such as banking and the law. Banking employments also carry a suggestion of large ownership, and this fact is doubtless accountable for a share of the prestige that attaches to the business. The profession of the law does not imply large ownership; but since no taint of usefulness, for other than the competitive purpose, attaches to the lawyer's trade, it grades high in the conventional scheme. Mercantile pursuits are only half-way reputable, unless they involve a large element of ownership and a small element of usefulness. They grade high or low somewhat in proportion as they serve the higher or the lower needs; so that the business of retailing the vulgar necessaries of life descends to the level of the handicrafts and factory labour. Manual labour, or even the work of directing mechanical processes, is, of course, on a precarious footing as regards respectability." (*Leisure Class*, p. 232.)

CHAPTER V

SOCIAL IMPLICATIONS OF A PREDATORY SYSTEM

WE are now in a position to enter on an inquiry into the broader and more various social implications of Veblen's economic interpretation of history. The term exploitation has a peculiar aptness as applied to the financial operations of absentee ownership. For it is a modern expression of the spirit of "exploit" and personal glory which in various forms has operated right through human history and can be traced in the earliest known forms of primitive society. In pursuit of this interpretation Veblen dives diligently into the new knowledge of ancient man disclosed by recent related studies of psychology and anthropology. From almost the earliest known types of primitive man in his dealings with his material and animal environment, the emergence of a prestigious and predatory life of exploit shows itself against the background of hard continuous productive labour required to furnish the needs of existence.

The fullest earlier statement of this case is

found in *The Theory of the Leisure Class*. This title does not, however, do full justice to the richness of an exposition which is concerned less with the emergence of a class of "idle rich" than with the early and continuous development of a radical distinction between ignoble forms of work and those more irregular non-productive activities summarized under the term exploit. Such a distinction is not found in the earliest human groups where abundant free fruits or easily cultivated food supplies maintain life on a peaceful basis of light labour. Even in such a society sexual and other enmities will doubtless give rise to combats, and some personal distinction between strength and weakness will differentiate alike individuals and sexes. But there will be no habitual sense of personal prowess as the dominant thought and fact. The quiet agricultural life where sufficient land is available need not breed that spirit of exploit which marks off a predatory class from the working members of a group. The pastoral life shows the beginnings of such a differentiation, combined, as it commonly is, with an unsettled mode of life and the occupation of disputed territory. The male here begins to assume direction and a certain dominion over the female, the latter being occupied with the care of children and the work about the temporary home. The hunting

IMPLICATIONS OF A PREDATORY SYSTEM

life, however, best illustrates the contrast, associated, as it commonly is, with fighting. "Both are of a predatory nature: the warrior and the hunter alike reap where they have not strewn. Their aggressive assertion of force and sagacity differs obviously from the women's assiduous and uneventful shaping of materials; it is not to be accounted productive labour, but rather an acquisition of substance by seizure"—"As the tradition gains consistency, the common sense of the community erects it into a canon of conduct; so that no employment and no acquisition is morally possible to the self-respecting man at this cultural stage except such as proceeds on the basis of prowess—force or fraud."[1]

Whereas in a peaceable primitive community the natural urge or propensity, which Veblen terms "the instinct of workmanship," will take effect in such sorts of productive work as give food for the spirit of emulation, it is not until the fighting-hunting stage that man is brought to despise routine labour in favour of the more emulative processes which testify to personal prowess. Booty, trophies, the fruits of conquest, become the accredited evidence of successful self-assertion, and goods obtained by such means count as more worthy than those got by labour.

[1] *Leisure Class*, p. 14.

"Labour acquires a character of irksomeness by virtue of the indignity imputed to it."[1] When slaves are taken by forcible capture, they not only become tokens of prowess in their captors, but they are converted into forced labourers whose work, added to that of the women, enables the men to free themselves more completely from productive labour and to employ their time and energy in dignified occupations. As barbarism advances into more settled society, two marked characteristics emerge. Other honourable types, besides those of the fighter and the hunter, assume prestigious value, viz., the ruler and the priest, medicine-man or wizard. Such men exercise moral or religious control over their fellow-tribesmen, performing invisible services attended by rites and ceremonies that are badges of their superiority. Freed from the indignity of labour, they extort a generous livelihood and leisure from the underlying population.

Associated with this development is a heightened regard for property. "The initial phase of ownership, the phase of acquisition by naive seizure and conversion, begins to pass into the subsequent stage of an incipient organization of industry on the basis of private property (in slaves); the trade develops into a more or less self-sufficing industrial

[1] Op. cit., p. 17.

IMPLICATIONS OF A PREDATORY SYSTEM

community; possessions thus come to be valued not so much as evidence of successful foray, but rather as evidence of the prepotence of the possessor of these goods over other individuals in the community. The invidious comparison now becomes primarily a comparison of the owner with the other members of the group."[1]

Here we find in Veblen an early expression of that radical distinction between work and ownership which differentiates his economics from the theory which finds in labour a natural right to the ownership of its product. To seize the product of another's labour and live on it, is by general admission a more dignified and "honourable" career than to earn one's bread by the sweat of one's brow. This is, of course, no cynical judgment, but a truthful expression of the way in which not only the possessing but the dispossessed classes feel and even think in the most highly civilized communities of to-day. The *naiveté* of the classical economics of the nineteenth century found the natural basis of property in productive labour, but its notions of production were derived from simple *a priori* imagination, not from anthropology and social psychology.

The prestige of ownership based not on labour but on prowess, the strong arm and the clever hand,

[1] Op. cit., p. 28.

treated by Veblen, branches out into innumerable modes of fruitful self-assertion using as instruments the various institutions of politics, religion, art, literature, sport and "society," which constitute the stuff called "civilization."

But before we can conveniently address ourselves to these attractive subjects, we must briefly outline some of the further and more recent developments of his primary distinction between work and predacity, with especial reference to the cultural aspects of that leisure which Veblen regards as the distinctive badge of the predatory life.

"During the predatory stage proper, and especially during the earlier stages of the quasi-peaceable development of industry that follow the predatory stage, a life of leisure is the readiest and most conclusive evidence of pecuniary strength and therefore of superior force; provided always that the gentleman of leisure can live in manifest ease and comfort. At this stage wealth consists chiefly of slaves, and the benefits accruing from the possession of riches and power take the form chiefly of personal service and the immediate products of personal services."[1] Leisure, however, does not imply mere idleness. It may find expression, and even a certain justification, in the development and practice of scholarly and artistic accom-

[1] Op. cit., p. 38.

IMPLICATIONS OF A PREDATORY SYSTEM

plishments and the acquisition of various forms of knowledge, provided that no directly biological utility attaches to these branches of culture. Dead languages are more honorific than living, not primarily, as may be contended, because of the higher value of their literary treasures, but because they are not tainted by any present practical utility. In other words, leisure and the pecuniary strength behind it, are well attested by the "accomplishments" of its possessors. So also with manners, "good form," polite and ceremonial observances. "Manners, we are told, are in part an elaboration of gesture, and in part they are symbolical and conventionalized survivals representing former acts of dominion or of personal service or of personal contact. In large part they are an expression of the relation of status—a symbolic pantomime of mastery on the one hand and of subservience on the other."[1]

The nature of the reprobation that attends a breach of good manners often approaches the sense of sacrilege and marks out the strong survival of an early and traditional code of behaviour which even rejects the present dominance of the *nouveaux riches* where their behaviour does not conform to the older traditions. "In the last analysis the value of manners lies in the fact that they are the voucher

[1] Op. cit., p. 47.

of a life of leisure. Therefore, conversely, since leisure is the conventionalized means of pecuniary repute, the acquisition of some proficiency in decorum is incumbent on all who aspire to a modicum of pecuniary decency."[1] Gentle birth and breeding come to play an exceedingly important part in the honorific life, because they imply a long-continued abstinence from any performance of productive services on the part of the well-born. A leisurely family life for many generations, even unattended by great possessions, will often outweigh in popular esteem the prestige of wealth and leisure recently acquired in trade or industry. Had Veblen possessed as intimate a knowledge of English as of American society, he could have enriched this theme by interesting illustrations, showing how the highly gainful occupations of banking and brewing acquired an earlier and higher prestige than ordinary factory work, how wholesale trade in general was severed in its gentility from retail trade, and how the owner of a retail business could acquire gentility by expanding into a company and removing his name from the shops he owned.

Conspicuous leisure, with its attendant conspicuous consumption, as the index of modern pecuniary power, finds its most intimate expression in the

[1] Op. cit., p. 49.

IMPLICATIONS OF A PREDATORY SYSTEM

ostentatious extravagance of the rich family life, its household, education, social entertainments, sports and recreations. When the family was in large measure productive of its food, clothing and other material requirements, the dominant male, enjoying a life of leisure qualified by brief exploits, set his wife along with his servants to the work necessary to produce these requisites. The family was a substantially self-sufficient productive group. But when industry took on organized and specialized forms outside the home and his pecuniary strength could be better employed in outside purchases, the element of leisure in its typical form of useless activities began to display itself in changes of the household life. The first of these was the withdrawal of the wife from most of her former productive functions. When marriage by capture had ceased and had been superseded by contractual unions within the group, the gentility of the wife's family may already have exempted her from productive work, so that she comes easily to occupy the more decorative role of the ruler and supervisor of an expensive household in which even the services of an increasing number of the servants are no longer productive or even useful, but are devoted to activities largely formal or ceremonial. The "lackey" is the type of this futile service, but the same quality of intrinsic disutility applies to the greater part of the household work, attendance upon idle members of the family, or the dusting and cleaning of numerous extravagantly furnished rooms. Here we enter the sphere of "conspicuous waste" which in modern times comes to reveal conspicuous leisure as a testimony to pecuniary power.

Though these characteristics are, of course, in fuller evidence among the rich, they have come to play, by snobbish imitation, an increasing part among the middle classes. Here ostentatious or honorific display is a more careful economy than among the rich. For it implies a considered preference for certain sorts of expense over others that may carry a higher real utility in the standard of living. The most striking modern example is found in the pecuniary efforts to keep a motor-car of reputable make and appearance, at a sacrifice of house-room or domestic service, or of the better education of the children. Here ostentatious consumption outcompetes ostentatious leisure, for the middle-class man will often put in a heavier week's work in his office or profession, in order to provide for the upkeep of his reputable car.

For the wife in every well-to-do class a larger part of her time and activities is allotted to "social duties." The term itself is worthy of consideration. It may doubtless be used to include the charitable

IMPLICATIONS OF A PREDATORY SYSTEM

services in which some wealthy women employ part of their spare time and money. The degradation which the word "charity" has suffered by this narrowing process that takes the heart out of it and reduces it to a monetary transfer marking the social superiority of the donor and the inferiority of the recipient, is itself a revealing commentary upon the class distinctions in society. But the ordinary use of the expression "social duties" is an abuse both of the term society and duty. For what constitutes "society" is a small circle of one's social equals and the duties exercised consist of visits and entertainments in which the polite formalities of conspicuous leisure are coupled with the display of conspicuous waste.

The ceremonial aspects of the leisured upper classes pass by facile imitation to the middle classes, as far as their pecuniary circumstances permit, so that lady-like occupations come more and more to carry the implication of disutility and freedom from the drudgery of household toil. Even where narrow circumstances compel the performance of some drudgery within the secret confines of the house, care is taken to secure as far as possible the appearance of ease and leisure in the outside life. Here dress is the most important expression of feminine status. Waste can more easily and effectually be expressed in this form than in any other. Veblen gives close attention to this aspect of conspicuous consumption in fashionable adornments. Jewellery is perhaps the most obvious and most assertive form of conspicuous waste in personal display. But skilful imitation, while not destroying its value in this role, has impaired its efficacy. In dress proper (or improper) the greatest prestige attaches to the large externals. This is where the presumptive high cost of the fur coat or the silk gown gets attention. Where such dress articles are able to preserve a scarcity value for an individual or a restricted grade of wearers, they still secure an important prestige. But the inventiveness and skill of modern industries, evoked by the very fact of this expensive rarity, evolves cheap and deceptive substitutes which extend these forms of personal display beyond the middle classes into almost every grade of working-class wives and daughters—one of the most levelling influences of our time. Veblen points out, however, some interesting features of personal adornment due to the penetration of the æsthetic sense into what might otherwise appear a mere welter of scarcity and eccentricity. So far as a natural or an educated sense of beauty comes to weigh with us, it makes more in the direction of simplicity than of loud expensiveness. "On this ground, among objects of use the simple and unadorned article is æsthetically the best. But since the pecuniary canon of reputability rejects the inexpensive in articles appropriated to individual consumption, the satisfaction for our craving for beautiful things must be sought by way of compromise. The canons of beauty must be circumvented by some contrivance that will give evidence of a reputably wasteful expenditure, at the same time that it meets the demands of our critical sense of the useful and the beautiful, or at least meets the demand of some habit which has come to do duty in that sense. Such an auxiliary sense of taste is the sense of novelty; and this latter is helped out in its surrogateship by the curiosity with which men view ingenious and puzzling contrivances."[1]

That novelty plays a determinant part in "fashion" is, of course, a familiar truth. How far this part is due to the curiosity Veblen names, or how far to the pecuniary interests of the reputable fashion-makers recognizing and coining this curiosity, remains a nice problem of economic balance. The two, no doubt, interact in the determination of changes in fashion.

When we come to consider how far machine production can displace skilled workmanship in making reputable goods, we are carried further into the economics of "good taste." A display

[1] Op. cit., p. 152.

of skilled workmanship is without doubt valued, partly on its own account, appealing to the æsthetic sense of the more cultivated classes. This honorific character is attested by certain elements of roughness or irregularity in execution—a certain "margin of crudeness." "This margin must never be so wide as to show bungling workmanship, since that would be evidence of low cost, nor so narrow as to suggest the ideal perfection attained only by the machine, for that would be evidence of low cost."[1]

This revolt against the standardized perfection of machine-products is aptly illustrated by the William Morris movement towards artistic book-making, where type, paper, illustration, binding material and work are all rescued from the prison of cheap uniformity. "The Kelmscott Press reduced the matter to an absurdity—as seen from the point of view of brute serviceability alone—by issuing books for modern use, edited with the obsolete spelling, printed in black letter and bound in limp vellum fitted with thongs."[2] The practice, current to-day, of publishing superior books in limited editions, exhibits accurately the economics of this reversion to the primitive.

But still more significant is the whole Arts and Crafts movement with its appeal to the spirit of

[1] Op. cit., p. 160.   [2] Op. cit., p. 163.

skilled workmanship and the lure of the rough edge. That the movement carries some element of producers' interest and sense of quality, as well as appealing to the finer taste of rich consumers who alone can afford to buy the dearer products of such work, may well be admitted. But the blend of costly display with the sentimentalism of a reversion to the antique is hardly compensated by the sort of manual skill and interest carried in such craftsmanship. The whole of this reversionary campaign is based upon a wrong conception of the work done by the ordinary workman under pre-machine industry. A few workers there exercised some fragments of skilled imitation and a sense of fine quality, but the bulk of the actual work was heavy toil carried to a degree which no well-regulated factory worker of to-day would tolerate. And since the whole movement can only survive by dependence on the patronage of a wealthy leisured class of consumers, it must be classed under Veblen's table of "conspicuous waste," with the thin æsthetic veneer that serves to give a cultural covering.

The simple maxim that "age gives respectability" easily develops into a recognition of the general doctrine of the conservatism of the respectable classes in their whole attitude towards life. The observation is expressed by

Veblen in the statement "Innovation is bad form."

All well-established customs, valuations and the institutions that embody them enjoy this reputability. They have not got to defend themselves on grounds of current utility: the prestige of the past protects them against obsolescence and displacement. Such protection is, of course, not absolute; obstructive or even useless customs and institutions must yield in course of time to newer, better, more obviously advantageous ones, but this process of reform is slow and wasteful. Sometimes the difficulties of gradual pacific reform are so great as to evoke a revolution, a rapid and often excessive clearance of past heritage.

But what chiefly concerns Veblen in dealing with this wasteful conservatism in modern times is the support it gives to the social domination of the wealthy class and in particular to the recent rulers of finance. For the defences of their pecuniary power thrown up by vested ownership extend to every sphere of organized activity, economic, political, religious, cultural, social, recreational. *"Panem et circenses"* was a crude early testimony to this defensive technique, designed to keep the people quiet and turn their thoughts away from active discontent with their lowly lot.

The term "designed," however, may easily

IMPLICATIONS OF A PREDATORY SYSTEM

convey an excessive consciousness of purpose. The true psychology of such procedure is nearly always more instinctive in its defensive action. An interesting modern instance has been the wide application of the "dole" for the relief of unemployment in England after the War when revolution was breaking out in many countries and seemed to threaten our social order. The humanitarian sentiment which operated as a chief conscious motive for the expense of an extended dole was a quite genuine motive. Yet honest history would rightly say that it served to buy off a revolutionary movement of which British democracy seemed capable. Though this could not be described as a fully conscious motive, some dim but real sense of its defensive value helped to bring about the policy.

CHAPTER VI

THE ECONOMICS OF EDUCATION

VEBLEN'S most distinctive intellectual work was the application of the psychology of the struggle by which the vested interests defend themselves against the threatened attacks of the under-classes to the various institutions that can be mobilized for defensive purposes. He gives great prominence to education in this struggle. We have already made allusion to the prestige accorded to dead languages and literature and other elements of reputable culture, as exhibitions of conspicuous waste. The educational time and energy they engage reduce the amount available for studies which carry some directly utilitarian services. But there is another meaning to this cultural preference. The antiquity of these studies makes them "safe." They are held to contain no knowledge or thinking that can feed a spirit of criticism and discontent with the respected institutions of to-day. Ancient history may, indeed, be pressed into the intellectual service of political revolution, as it was by French rebels in the eighteenth century.

But it is far more innocuous than a veracious history of modern times which might disclose the actual processes by which the wealth and power of the ruling classes were attained and direct dangerous thoughts and feelings into attempts to secure a more equitable sharing of those goods. In most English schools this danger is met in two ways; first, by beginning a long way back in national history and occupying so much time with the earlier epochs so that most pupils never get far into the nineteenth century; secondly, by confining attention to the lives and doings of the kings and ruling classes, their wars and high politics, so that the lives and doings of the common people are almost ignored. In American schools the same result is attained by the concentration of attention upon the founding of the Colonies, the War of Independence, and a worshipful study of the Constitution and the political and economic expansion of the country up to the Civil War. Intellectual and moral controversies which might underlie these political and military struggles are not deemed fit for the young scholar, whose mind should be fed with a diet of established facts which shall constitute a stock of knowledge. Controversy would only confuse his mind and perhaps stir a spirit of sceptical inquiry which might be turned upon current issues.

Where the elements of civics, politics and economics are introduced into some bolder schools, care must be taken to keep them inoffensive by confining them to descriptive information, or, if any controversial issue is introduced, to a balanced statement of the *pros* and *cons*. While it is admitted by most thoughtful teachers that a living interest in history and in social institutions would be best evoked by an intelligible account of current happenings and the present-day working of these institutions, the evolution of which would carry the student backward into the earlier stages of the society in which he lived, this rational process is banned by its very merit of rationality. For though educationalists will admit, somewhat reluctantly, that children should be taught to use their minds and not merely have knowledge pumped into them, very little is done to stir and exercise their reasoning faculty. This defect in teaching is no doubt partly due to the fact that teachers themselves have seldom been taught to reason and would find this training of the young difficult and uncongenial, but chiefly because reasoning on controversial topics would cause misunderstanding among parents and school trustees and interfere with the peaceful career of the teacher.

This neglect of all serious attempt to teach school children to use their minds otherwise than in

THE ECONOMICS OF EDUCATION

acquiring information and the elementary arts necessary for the performance of their social duties, such as reading, writing and arithmetic, becomes a more serious defect when the higher stage of education is reached. Here Veblen may rank as an expert who has tasted and tested, as learner and teacher, the curriculum and methods of instruction of American colleges and universities of many ranks and in several states. The final record of his experience, fortified by wide information from other accredited sources, is set forth in his book entitled *The Higher Learning*. We have already seen that two distinguishable though closely related origins are found everywhere embedded in his sociology, the interpretation of human conduct in terms of economic materialism and the play of the psychological factor termed "idle curiosity." The institutions for Higher Learning in America he shows as a cockpit of struggle between these two forces or motives. The play of this struggle is highly complex, subtle and only half-conscious, and is carried on, partly in the classes and the teaching faculty, partly, in the administrative control by the President and the Board of Teachers, and, behind both these direct agencies, in the circle of rich charitable donors and the politicians who regulate State subsidies.

In setting forth this play of disturbing or ill-ordered controls it is necessary to realize how large is the place of this higher education in the social life of the country. Taking first the financial aspect, a larger amount and a larger proportion of the income of the country is spent on higher education than in any other country and the proportion of fixed endowments is smaller than elsewhere. Thus education, as a pecuniary proposition, occupies more attention, and its finance is more closely dependent upon current conditions of economic life. In times of depression, like the present, universities have suffered heavily and not a few colleges have been forced to close down for lack of funds.

But this financial aspect of education is chiefly of concern to Veblen in its bearing upon the struggle of "idle curiosity," or disinterested learning, to hold its own against the invasion of utilitarian influences in the shape of technical and professional studies. Admitting that in the beginning it was the biological and other real or imagined needs of man that laid the foundation of the sciences, and that the earlier schools and universities were dominated by the practical requirements of law, medicine, theology and engineering, he argues that intellectual progress has demanded a severance between utilitarian and disinterested studies and that, though contacts must always be maintained between the two, they should be organized in separate departments. The intrinsic worth of disinterested studies has usually enabled them to hold their own and often to gain ground over the distinctly utilitarian studies even where the formal dominance of the latter existed.

"Under the regime of unmitigated pragmatic aims that ruled the earlier days of the European universities, the pursuit of knowledge for its own sake was carried on as a work of scholarly supererogation by men whose ostensibly sole occupation was the promulgation of some accredited line of salutary information. Frequently it had to be carried on under some colourable masquerade of practicality. And yet so persistent has the spirit of idle curiosity proved to be, and so consonant with the long-time demands even of the laity, that the dissimulation and smuggling in of disinterested learning has gone on even more openly and at an ever-increasing rate of gain; until in the end, the attention given to scholarship and the non-utilitarian sciences in these establishments has come far to exceed that given to the practical disciplines for which the several faculties were originally installed."[1]

The position in America is, however, somewhat confused. The early colleges were continuations

[1] *Higher Learning*, p. 37.

of the schools and had no distinctively professional and utilitarian bias. But the later growth of universities has made difficulties in the educational system. Veblen sees a deep discrepancy between the college with its undergraduates and a true university. For though the latter has often formally incorporated the former, the college standards and methods of control are really alien to the higher learning and the work of independent research which properly belong to a university. Though the two departments in a university may be kept apart so far as the teaching function is concerned, the part taken by the professional and technical teachers in the policy and financial control of the university is detrimental to disinterested learning. He finds two faults, first with the incorporation of undergraduate and graduate teaching in the same institution; secondly, with the inclusion of professional and technical work in a university.

Though the power of the financier, whether exercised by private donations or by political pressures, might seem at first sight likely to quench the spirit of disinterested learning and to convert the system of higher education into methods of research endowed with immediate practical utility, Veblen finds no sufficient grounds to support this judgment. He finds the instinct of idle curiosity endowed with a survival power so strong that it

THE ECONOMICS OF EDUCATION

can hold its own against the utilitarian demands. A university comes more and more to be "a seat of the higher learning, a corporation for the pursuit of knowledge." "Nothing is felt to be so irremediably vicious in academic policy as a conscious bias, religious, political, conventional or professional, in so far as it touches that quest of knowledge that constitutes the main interest of the university."[1]

By virtue of this genuinely scientific force, supported by a strong widespread idealism which everywhere tempers the practical strain in the American character, Veblen considers that any university which plays fast and loose with its cultural interests must fall into hopeless discredit. But the struggle to preserve its virtue is a wasteful one, especially in those State Universities whose finances lie at the mercy of political bosses and where the professional organizations are often dominant in the administrative posts. "For a generation past while the American universities have been coming into line as seminaries of the higher learning, there has gone on a wide-reaching substitution of laymen in the place of clergymen on the governing boards."—"So that the discretionary control in matters of university policy now rests finally in the hands of business men."[2] At first sight it might appear that this change would

[1] Op. cit., p. 39.   [2] Op. cit., p. 64.

imply greater liberty of thought and teaching for the academic staff. For clergymen would be likely to interfere more in the making of the curriculum and would demand orthodoxy in the teachers, whereas business men would have no intellectual axe to grind and would confine themselves to the legitimate work of trustees, the management of the estate and the provisions of the necessary current finances. It is, indeed, held to be desirable for a growing university with increasing pecuniary needs to have upon its governing body a few wealthy business men whose local patriotism may help to furnish endowments, or provide large subscriptions to meet emergencies. But the belief that the business management of a university can be separated from the appointment of teachers, the selection of subjects of study and the methods of teaching, upon which the efficiency of such an institution must depend, is unjustified. The pecuniary surveillance exercised by a board of business men "serves in the main to an interference with the academic work, the merits of which these men of affairs on the governing board are in no special degree qualified to judge."[1]

Such business control, reflecting, as to some extent it must, the personal sentiments and interests of its representatives, is certain to be conservative

[1] Op. cit., p. 65.

in regard to such branches of instruction as concern themselves with politics and economics and also other subjects fraught with present-day controversial topics. For the conservatism of the pecuniary class is by no means confined to banns upon radical teaching in economic theory. By an instinctive sense of the interdependence of all subjects of current importance it extends its protective influence to the teaching of law, ethics and religion, and even to such sciences as biology and psychology which may harbour doctrines disturbing to the modern mind. For though, as we have seen, the business man, himself directly concerned with the successful conduct of practical affairs, is not averse from the spread of disinterested culture as a decorative element of civilized life, this culture must not be allowed to trespass on the fields of current conduct so as to stir an unrest which may threaten the stability of American institutions or customary standards. In other words, so long as intellectual culture remains "disinterested," distinctively "idle," it is to be encouraged as a mode of conspicuous leisure which America can afford to an ever-widening proportion of her population. But if culture becomes "interested" in the sense of contributing to processes of thought which stimulate reforms and reconstructions in the political, economic, legal and social institutions of

America, such culture must be carefully suppressed. As Veblen shows, such suppression is no easy task, for as all history shows, ideas endowed with vitality have an inconvenient way of reappearing in virtue of the element of truth they may contain. But if they cannot be killed, they may be kept under by judicious surveillance. The universities of America within recent years have, both in their teaching and their extra-mural activities, been subjected to increasing interference with liberty of thought and speech. For the post-War years have given a potent stimulus both to the courage of liberal thinkers and to the apprehensions of conservatives. The increasing part played in America as elsewhere by Government and the State in social-economic legislation and administration has brought into the foreground of consciousness issues of great moment, to the discussion of which the advocates of new theories and new reforms have applied themselves with vigour, while the defenders of the political-economic established doctrines and practices have utilized every available weapon of repression which the armoury of legal and illegal forces contains.

In short, so soon as the higher learning ceases to be merely decorative and begins to show an interfering spirit, it is denounced by business men as useless or worse, and Governing Boards exercise

THE ECONOMICS OF EDUCATION

directly, through financial controls, or indirectly through pressure on the Administration, a censorship as effective as they know how to make it. Thus the natural opposition between science and business and between the scientific side of industry and the pecuniary side assumes a sharp antagonism. This natural opposition is thus expressed by Veblen.

"Science has to do with the opaquely veracious sequence of cause and effect, and it deals with the facts of this sequence without mental reservations or ulterior purposes of expediency. Business enterprise proceeds on ulterior purposes and calculations of expediency; it depends on shrewd expedients and lives on the margin of error, on the fluctuating margin of human miscalculation. The training given by these two lines of endeavour —science and business—is wholly divergent; with the notorious result that for the purposes of business enterprise the scientists are the most ignorant, gullible and incompetent class in the community. They are not only passively out of touch with the business spirit, out of training by neglect, but they are also positively trained out of the habit of mind indispensable to business enterprise. The converse is true of the men of business affairs."[1]

This opposition would not matter so much if each side kept itself to itself. But when the scientist

[1] Op. cit., p. 77.

through his sciences of economics and politics begins to invade the world of business, while the business man responds, in the ways above described by directing or dictating the sorts of teaching and the teachers employed in the offending studies, the confusion and the peril to the higher learning become serious.

But the business control of higher learning is by no means confined to the action of the Governing Boards. It pervades the Administration. The President, or chief Executive, plays the chief, almost the sole, part, in the making of a successful university. But that "success" tends more and more to be computed, not in terms of disinterested learning, but rather in terms of competitive prestige, as measured by intake and output of students, magnitude of buildings and other material equipment and in reputable social and athletic reputation by means of clubs, fraternities and other instruments of genteel dissipation. Now this sort of success depends largely upon the training, selection and activity of a good Executive. Veblen finds a resemblance between the normal academic Executive and the typical professional politicians. In both are found the qualities of a " 'business-like' facility in the management of affairs, an engaging address and a fluent command of language before a popular audience and what is called 'optimism'

—"a serene and voluble loyalty to the current conventionalities and a conspicuously profound conviction that all things are working out for good, except for such untoward details as do not visibly conduce to the vested advantage of the well-to-do business men under the established law and order."[1] University employment in the administrative rather than the learned side is the best preparation for such an executive post, though some quasi-scholarly reputation has its value. Although by tradition the President exercises no formal authoritative control over teachers and teaching, occupying the position of Chairman at the meetings of the faculty, he does in fact determine all important issues of policy and personnel. His position resembles the description once given by Lord Rosebery in the early 'nineties when asked to define the standing of Great Britain in Egypt. "We are in a position to give authoritative advice to the Khedive." The fact that he is the employer of the teaching and administrative staffs is the first evidence of the intrusion of business methods into university life. But if his first duty is that of keeping his faculty under proper control, probably the more important part of his work consists in the acquisition of reputable publicity for his university.

Though not directly conducive to the scholarly

[1] Op. cit., p. 245.

or even the financial strength of his university, popular addresses on a variety of occasions, such as commencements, inaugurations, club meetings, church festivals, are important parts of the work of an executive who shall advertise his university successfully and win the approval of big business men prepared to find the necessary financial aids either privately or through State appropriations. This competitive aspect has come to play a larger part in recent years. With it has come an increased tendency towards the practical professional studies and what Veblen terms the decline of disinterested scholarship. For neither the pecuniary potentates, whose goodwill must be sought and held, nor the larger public, appealed to by advertising oratory, are true believers in the higher learning. What they want is training for business and professional life with close relations between theoretic science and the technical progress which alone can justify expenditure upon disinterested learning.

This complex government of universities with the standardization of its constituent schools on "a mechanically specified routine and scale" is anathema to Veblen. He would like to see the abolition both of the governing board and the central executive in order that the teaching units might be free to follow their own intellectual devices. "Left to themselves the several schools would have to take care each of its own affairs and guide its endeavours by the exigencies of its own powers and purposes, with such regard to intercollegiate comity and courtesy as would be required by the substantial relations then subsisting between them, by virtue of their common employment in academic work."[1] "Indeed, there might even be ground to hope that, on the dissolution of the trust, the underlying academic units would return to that ancient footing of small-scale parcelment and personal communion between teacher and student that once made the American college, with all its handicap of poverty, chauvinism and denominational bias, one of the most effective agencies of scholarship in Christendom."[2]

This hope of the return to intellectual sanity is not, however, supported by recent experience. For Veblen cites two instances, in the Middle-West and the Far-West where the initial purpose of establishing "a seminary of the higher learning as distinct from an assembly of vocational schools," under conditions that seemed very favourable in regard both to finance and directive personnel, gave way "under pressure of circumstances" to "the ubiquitous craving for statistical magnitude and the consequent felt need of conciliatory publicity," lapsing into the prevailing utilitarian type.

[1] Op. cit., p. 281. [2] Op. cit., p. 284.

In other words, the dominance of large-scale finance entering the field of education asserts its control over the machinery and output of cultural values, subduing to distinctively professional ends the craving for knowledge and disinterested thinking which otherwise might either direct mental activity into useless curiosity, or might employ it in speculative or active processes of social reform.

The attention given by Veblen to the corrupting influences exercised by finance and politics upon the cultural liberty of universities must not, however, lead his readers to suppose that he regarded the battle for disinterested education as lost. For this corruption is linked up with a financial dominion which in his view does not express the permanent forces in American civilization. This further hope finds the following expression in his Introductory Chapter: "But there is at the same time equally prevalent through the community a long-term line of another kind, such as will not enduringly tolerate the sordid effects of pursuing an educational policy that looks mainly to the main chance, and universally makes the means of life its chief end. By virtue of this long-term idealistic drift, any seminary of learning that plays fast and loose with the cultural interests entrusted to its keeping loses caste and falls out of the running."[1]

[1] Op. cit., p. 42.

CHAPTER VII

THE FIELD OF POLITICS

I

THOUGH the place given by Veblen to economic forces in the determination of the political and other social systems and activities was one of prime importance, he did not, as we have seen, ignore other influences which help to mould social conduct. For there are many instincts, urges, desires, which belong to the natural equipment of human beings in their relations to one another and which are shaped and authorized by traditional and environmental influences. Some of those may be at times more potent determinants of social behaviour than the activities directed to economic ends of food, shelter, comfort and the like. The strength of economic motives lies in the greater continuity of the biological needs they serve and in the dominant part they play in critical moments of emergency. When the economic activities pass under the central financial control which Veblen finds operative in his country, and to a large extent throughout the civilized world, this continuity and skilled guidance assume a higher measure of consciousness, taking on the form of a business policy. If this be admitted, the very use of the term "policy" brings us into the neighbourhood of politics, and the politician draws close to the business man.

Now the original keynote of American politics is found in the restricted governmental powers vested either in the Federal or the State Governments, or conversely in the liberty of the citizen from public interference with his right to regulate his life and employ his capacity for his own ends. The conception of private property and the right to obtain it by any lawful means are also deeply embedded in this American mentality, and the Laws under the Constitution are exceedingly liberal in the freedom they have accorded to citizens to utilize the opportunities presented by a land of large undeveloped natural resources. So long as free land of a cultivable quality lay open to pioneer settlers of American stock or to European immigrants, this condition of liberty and opportunity was fulfilled sufficiently to support the traditional belief. The farming settler was not yet brought under the yoke of capitalism. The growth of organized industries in the growing cities of the East took up, however, an ever-increasing proportion of the tide of immigrants from Southern and Eastern Europe, converting them into a cheap proletariat available for profitable business enterprise. Though wages were low for this unskilled labour, the growth of population, farming and industrial, was large enough to support an expanding market for goods, and though considerable waste occurred, there was no need to pursue a policy of restricted production. This era of economic and political liberty continued until the development of the new Middle-Western and Western cities began to bulk big in the national economy, and the farm-settlers began to come under the control of the country-town banks and the new railroads. The development of great coal, iron and oil areas by cheap labour brought considerable districts and their populations under the rigorous control of owners and managers who found it advisable to utilize the legal and political machinery at their disposal to tighten this control. When land and housing came to be owned by employing corporations, it was inevitable that their legal rights should enable them so to control the conditions of labour, as to prevent any effective organized resistance of the workers to a system of "peonage" closely resembling slavery in many areas. Where the State constitution and existing laws did not afford them the full powers of economic control which they needed, they were able by controlling the political machinery to make the additional laws they wanted and to secure their favourable administration by the police, judicial and other official instruments.

But the more typical evolution of the financial power and its use of politics are traceable in the mushroom growth of new cities and of the smaller country towns. For here lay the great opportunities of rapid money-making for those who could command financial capital. Rising land values and "public utilities," connected with the economic developments of new towns and cities, were the obvious sources of unearned gain. The gain took two forms; first, that of increasing speculative land values, where pecuniary magnates could trade upon the future, making immense profits by transfers discounting the results of further growth of population and their needs; secondly the direct gains from a monopolistic operation of the public utilities, roads, tramways, lighting, and other services which helped to boost their land values. This order of money-making demanded a complete control of the "franchises" conveying the legal right to obtain and exercise these monopolies. For it was important for the landowners to determine the detailed lie of the streets, lighting and other services in relation to their lands, as well as the control of the finances involved in these processes. Veblen regards the country town, of whose operations he had so intimate a personal experience, as the chief school for the business-politician. There little groups of Yankee business men took charge.

"This politico-pecuniary enterprise in municipal prerequisites is a case of joint-action rather than of collective action" since "each and several of the participants, overt and covert, takes part as a strategist or diplomatic agent for his own pecuniary interests."[1] This alliance of politics with industry and finance, with its attendant graft and bribery, was, of course, no novelty in American history. But with the rapid evolution of the city, and the development of the key industries of transport and power, it assumed dimensions which were destined to transform the whole economic structure of the nation. When public offices, legislative, judicial, administrative, were generally recognized as a means of private graft, and big business was aware that it could purchase the legal rights conducive to its profitable working, a condition of things arose which existed in no other civilized country. Corruption is found in most countries, but nowhere upon such a scale, for nowhere else have the opportunities of operating public utilities

[1] Dorfman, p. 342.

and key industries for private profit been so numerous and so lucrative. Moreover, the notoriety of graft and corruption has kept honourable citizens out of politics so much that common honesty in public affairs is not expected of party politicians, and the two dominant parties in each state and city have been regarded as engaged less in expounding or carrying out opposed political principles or policies than in securing for themselves "the spoils of office."

The full implications of this corrupt connexion did not appear before the 'nineties. For it was then that the strategic significance of the "trust," the combine, the holding company, and other distinctively financial instruments became evident. For then the technique of modern industry in factory, mine, railway, had made such large advances that the difficulties of small or even big competing businesses to market the full output of which they were capable at prices that were profitable, began to be increasingly apparent. Lincoln Steffens and other social detectives made startling revelations of the corrupt relations between big business and municipal and state politics in many parts of America, while the formation of the Standard Oil Trust, and later on the so-called Steel Trust, furnished conspicuous examples of the displacement of competition by monopoly

THE FIELD OF POLITICS

in key industries. The difficulties in preserving that spirit of free competitive enterprise and equality of economic opportunity, which lay at the heart of American democracy, under a federal Constitution so ill-equipped for dealing with industry and commerce on a national scale, now became apparent. The extension of federal power under the Inter-State Commerce Act was utilized as a check upon the new "combines" and an attempt was made to hamper their structure and limit their area of activity. But their control of politics in New Jersey their "favourite state" for incorporation, with the practical impossibility of so amending the Federal Constitution as to secure for the nation the defensive powers which every other civilized nation possesses to stop economic oppression, enabled the new financial control of big business to pursue its course with little difficulty. Obsolete or obsolescent constitutions and laws governed by eighteenth century conceptions of rights of property enabled the big corporation lawyers to defeat most attempts to curb the monopoly powers of the combines. No political party preserved the will and the power to press for the radical constitutional reforms essential to curb the abuses of the organizers of big business and their financial controllers. Though the oppressed sections of the farming and industrial population made several efforts at political organization, they were impotent against the older party machines. The widely diverse conditions of land-ownership and cultivation in forty-eight separate states rendered effective co-operation of farm-workers impracticable, while the powerfully organized aristocracy of labour under the A.F.L. denied all effective representation to the lower grades of industrial workers, mostly of recent immigrant origin in the North, negroes or "mean" whites in the South.

Moreover, so slow is the infiltration of new truths into the mass-mind, that even in the earlier years of this century the traditional belief that America was a land of equal opportunities where every man of grit and energy could rise into a higher economic and social grade, was still generally prevalent. Some notorious instances served to maintain a creed which was steadily passing into a fable. Though liberty and equality were gradually shrinking, with the disappearance of free land and of free competitive enterprise in most branches of profitable industry and commerce, the relatively high standard of living among the skilled workers and the hopes of the new immigrants whose wages, though lower, were generally above the level of the country they had quitted, served to conceal the darker features of the new economic situation. The Great War was an "eye-opener" in America as elsewhere. Its years of strenuous production, first for loans to the allies then for actual participation in the war, taught several plain lessons. The enormous productive waste in normal times was made manifest by the great increase of output during the war years. Some of this increased output and income went in higher wage-rates to the workers and higher prices to the farmers. But the great expansion of profits to the capitalist-financiers, the vast fortunes made, first out of the loans, then out of the arming of the American forces by the groups in pecuniary control, were the most dramatic feature of war economics. But even more important was the revelation of a Federal Government which, disregarding all ordinary constitutional and legal rules, fastened public controls upon all essential industries and endeavoured to make the whole production of the country subordinate to public policy. Though this assertion of State socialism did not outlast the War, it left certain results upon the mentality of a people which hitherto had never regarded socialism as a serious proposition for America. The little groups of professed socialists among the European immigrants from Central and Eastern Europe, and among the radical-intellectuals of the well-to-do classes, carried no weight in practical politics. But war-experience showed that the economic liberty of America was inadequate to deal with a great national emergency when the productive resources of the country must be put to full uses and directed by a common purpose. Though much waste, error and incompetence were disclosed in the course of this war-experiment, the net result seemed to show that, given a strong national incentive, the economic system could be utilized under public control so as to work far more effectively than under normal "free" competitive conditions. This at any rate was a lesson of the war impressed upon the mind of large numbers of Americans. It would, however, almost certainly have faded away, if the subsequent peace era had not in a few years' time produced an "emergency of peace" with an appeal almost as powerful as the emergency of war. Though Veblen did not live far enough into the era of depression which still holds America in its grip to realize its full significance, he had in his later writings, especially in *The Nature of Peace*, presented the probability, almost the inevitability of such a depression. "The new dispensation offers two new factors bearing upon this business-like need of a sagacious sabotage, or rather it brings a change of coefficients in two factors already familiar in business management; a greater need, for gainful business, of resorting to such limitation of traffic; and a greater facility of ways and means for enforcing the needed restriction. So, it is confidently to be expected that in the prospective piping time of peace the advance in the industrial arts will continue at an accelerated rate; which may confidently be expected to affect the practicable increased production of merchantable goods; from which it follows that it will act to depress the price of those goods; from which it follows that if a profitable business is to be done in the conduct of productive industry, a greater degree of contrivance than before will have to be exercised in order not to let prices fall to an unprofitable figure; that is to say, "the permissible outlet must be held short of the productive capacity of such industry by a wider margin than before."[1] On

---

[1] Many economists will quite reasonably question the assumption made by Veblen here as elsewhere that an increasing output cannot be marketed without such a fall of prices as will make its full production unprofitable. They will point out, first, that Veblen assumes that the money income needed to buy the increasing output does not grow at a corresponding rate. But why should it not? If the increasing output is due to improved plant and organization, though the workers may not get increased money wages for their share in production, profits, interest, rent will be paid more, and this increase of "unearned" income has an increased purchasing power sufficient to purchase the increased output. Secondly, even if selling prices do fall, it does not necessarily follow that it will no longer pay to produce the marginal part of the output. For the monetary costs of production for each unit of the enlarged supply may fall with the fall in over-heads and in wage-cost sufficiently to counteract any fall of selling prices due to elasticity of demand.

I do not think Veblen anywhere fully faces the problem here

the other hand, it is well known out of the experience of the past few decades that a larger coalition of invested capital, controlling a larger proportion of the output, can more effectively limit the supply to a salutary maximum, such as will afford reasonable profits.—The outcome to be looked for should apparently be such an effective recourse to capitalistic sabotage as will neutralize any added advantage that might otherwise accrue to the community from its continued improvements in technology."[1]

Though it would be foolish to contend that the prolonged depression with its admitted wastes of plant and labour has won any widespread assent among economists for Veblen's doctrine of capitalist sabotage as a conscious policy, there is a growing acceptance of the view that, since capitalism no longer pretends to be on a basis of free competition, the interests of the consumer in an increasing output at lower prices, as the fruit of technological progress, are not safeguarded. It is equally clear that anti-trust laws and other legal attempts to check monopoly and to regulate

raised. It can only be solved by considerations relating to the distribution of money income, in purchasing power between its two uses, the buying of final goods (spending) and the buying of new capital goods through saving and investment. Rejecting the Marxist explanation which shows how large surplus income induces over-saving and under-spending, Veblen provides himself with no sufficient alternative explanation of his assumption that the pecuniary controllers of industry are compelled in the interests of profit to sabotage industry.

[1] *The Nature of Peace*, p. 341.

THE FIELD OF POLITICS

selling prices and wages cannot succeed, even if the Federal Court of Appeal permits them to function. Though the recognition of those facts has undoubtedly given some new support to the ideas and policy of socialism both among intellectuals, technicians and workers, there is no reason to believe that either State-socialism or any large scheme of public planning is feasible. The chief obstacle is not the faith in competitive individual enterprise, for that admittedly is disappearing over an ever-wider area of industry and commerce. It is the discredit attached to the State and its officials, arising from the revelations of corrupt practices in municipal, state and federal politics that bars the way even to such limited State-socialism as is practised in Western Europe. In theory the remedy for capitalist sabotage and for the political graft connected with public franchises would be that the democracy should, through its official instruments, take over those financial and industrial powers which are abused for private profiteering. But how can sober and informed American citizens trust their legislators, their "spoils" officials, their judges and their police with the conduct of big business so as to secure honesty and efficiency? Though it be admitted that the corrupt arrangements between politicians and profiteers are attributable to the vast and numerous opportunities for making quick big gains under private enterprise, the poisoning of officialdom which has attended this process makes it unreasonable to expect that State-socialism or any public planning would be worked successfully. So "better to bear the ills we have, than fly to others that we know not of" is the current sentiment of the average man.

Moreover, the line of analysis taken by Veblen does not commend democratic socialism as the remedy. For, as we have seen, though he gives a guarded acceptance to the doctrine of socially created values, his stress on the opposition between technician and financier prohibits the acceptance of class-war in the Marxian sense and of a subsequent economic peace based on proletarian rule. By attributing modern productive progress to the inventive and administrative energy of technicians and "engineers," he not unnaturally finds his remedy for sabotage and waste in an economic regime where the real power is taken away from those who abuse it and given to organizations of technicians who shall use it for the enlargement of production and the consequent gain of the community. But such a solution along lines of Guild socialism is not socialism in any proper sense, nor is it consistent with the democracy of American political life. Were it feasible, it would furnish no criterion by which the relative importance of different industries could be assumed. It could not properly be left to the engineers of each several industry to determine how much productive energy should go into increasing its particular line of goods. Though in one or two places Veblen seems to recognize that some correlating body will be required, representing the several industries, he does not discover or discuss the principles of valuation to be applied in order to apportion productive power to the wants or needs of the consuming public. The consumer is left out of the economic picture, the citizen out of the political, if indeed it can be said that Veblen presents the political picture at all. Yet an alternative political control must somehow be secured, if a capitalism that has passed from a competitive into a corporate form is to be rescued from the collapse into which it appears to have passed, as a result of modern financial operations. If that political control demands such reforms of electoral and other governmental machinery as shall raise the efficiency and the morals of legislative, administrative and judicial bodies to the required level, it would seem that these reforms stand in the foreground of any progressive movement in America. Veblen rightly dwells upon the difficulties placed in the way of all political and other social reforms by the survival of traditional ideas and sentiments. One of these is the surviving notion of "equality" as a root principle of democratic government. This had a *raison d'être* in eighteenth-century political thinking, because of the needed protest against class-domination in politics, economics and every social sphere of action. It also received support from the religious maxim that all men were equal "in God's sight." But it is notoriously untrue that men are equal in any sense that counts for life in this world. Yet Adam Smith lent support to the notion, perhaps in protest against the class-obstruction of his age. In America the idea has lingered on, partly through constant repetitions of the trinitarian formula of "liberty, equality and fraternity," partly because until recent times the power of adapting himself to any new demand or opportunities appeared to imply that for any practical purpose any man was as good as any other (with certain marked exceptions). The present writer, in conversation with William Jennings Bryan, was amazed to find the latter defending the advantages of a spoils system which put into office a fresh lot of untrained men with each change of government, by asserting that the new officials would bring with them a stock of knowledge and ability as good as that of those who were displaced. A good American could turn his hand to any job and put a strictly "common" sense into its execution. No doubt this belief is decaying, but it is slow to die, and an exaggerated sentiment of equality still blocks the way to efficient government.

If socialism of the proletarian order seemed inadmissible to Veblen, so did its revolutionary alternative fascism. For such a breach with the spirit and the forms of democracy is scarcely conceivable for America, Britain, or even France, where the dynastic conception of government has perished. The fear of socialism or communism which brought dictatorship in Italy and Germany, where democratic policy had never been firmly founded, could not go further than strengthen the hold which the propertied and business classes have always exercised over the representative forms of government. The endowment of a Hitler or a Mussolini with dictatorial powers, involving the cancelment of the political and economic liberties of ordinary men and women, could not take place in nations so refractory to personal discipline and so resentful of invasions of their ordinary rights as Americans or British. The control of internal politics in these countries must, therefore, continue to be conducted by the masterclass, by manipulation of the democratic machinery, rather than by its supersession, and the skilled arts of modern propaganda must be used so as to give a specious appearance to the contrived "consent of the governed." Moreover, the temper of the secretly ruling minority in these countries is so modified by traditional sentiments and by a genuine humanitarianism as to make the reversion to the barbaric practices of Germany and Italy inconceivable. For, though many isolated and particular acts of forcible abuse of power may be cited to the contrary, it remains true that the adoption and practice of democratic policies for many generations has made impossible a revolutionary reversion to medievalism. Under these circumstances even the grave emergency of prolonged economic depressions, though menacing internal peace and order, does not seem likely to cause a class-war which shall overthrow the existing political and economic system.

II

On the Nature of Peace exhibits a departure from the distinctively economic interpretation of politics in its handling of international relations that is somewhat unexpected. Veblen sets out very clearly the modern changes which make at first sight for pacific internationalism, the shrinkage of space and time under new methods of travel and communication, the increasing mobility of men and goods, the growth of material standardization in methods of production and consumption, and the advantages to each country of specialization on the basis of its best natural resources for the world market. Against this expansion of earlier Cobdenite doctrine and policy, he sets the barriers to free trade and mobility of populations which economic nationalism sets up, the tariffs, subsidies, embargoes and other obstacles. In his analysis of the causes of this nationalism, he surprisingly ignores the Marxian explanation, accepted by Lenin in his work on *Imperialism* and by not a few economists in America and Britain. Economic nationalism, on the one hand, as a policy of national self-sufficiency or isolation, imperialism, on the other hand, as a struggle for foreign markets and for backward countries as places for investment and development, are explained by Marx as the inevitable products of just such a tendency of capitalism towards excessive production as Veblen imputes to his financial domination. They are organized endeavours of capitalist groups to utilize the diplomatic and forcible powers of their national government for commercial and financial expansion by the subjugation and annexation or "peaceful penetration" of areas possessing raw materials for development and populations for import and export trade. Veblen is curiously reticent on the evidences which history affords for this economic explanation of national-imperialism. Not that he ignores the part which certain capitalist interests, in particular the makers of armaments, play in promoting hostility between nations and impeding the movement towards pacific internationalism. But, in his *Imperial Germany* and still more clearly in his *Nature of Peace*, he goes behind economic causation into the psychology of patriotism for his explanation. Perhaps it may be held that his devotion to the cause of "financial sabotage" led him to turn a blind eye to the Marxian view. For financial sabotage, or restriction of output, demands a non-expansive market as a condition of its profitable application, and this is more convincing if the possibility of an expanding world market is left out of account. Yet the case of Britain during the greater part of the nineteenth century should have made it evident that no curtailment of production was needed in capitalist industry so long as large foreign markets were available for the surplus goods which could not be sold to ill-paid workers in their country of origin. Apart from interruptions due to war, pestilence and famine, or to errors in calculation or in monetary policy, the early expansion of British capitalism called for no "sabotage" in the interests of owners or financiers.

Peace, or the effective internationalism in the spheres of business and of government, which Veblen desiderates, is blocked, he finds, by obsolescent feelings of patriotism based not on economic but on distinctively sentimental or emotional lines. "The patriotic spirit is a spirit of emulation, evidently, at the same time that it is emulation shot through with a sense of solidarity. It belongs under the general caption of sportsmanship, rather than of workmanship. Now every enterprise in sportsmanship is bent on an invidious success, which must involve as its major purpose defeat and humiliation of some competitors, whatever else may be comprised in its aim.— Patriotism is of a contentious complexion, and finds its full expression in no other outlet than war-like enterprise; its highest and final appeal is for the death, damage, discomfort and destruction of the party of the second part."[1]

This account of the "patriotic animus" as a collective development of the "*sacro egoismo*,"

---

[1] *Nature of Peace*, p. 33. This analysis will be challenged on two heads. The spirit of sportsmanship, it will be maintained, is not primarily or chiefly one of "invidious success" but of the organized play interest: it does not rejoice in the "humiliation" of the beaten man or team. Secondly, though patriotism may find its supreme test in war, as a sentiment it comprises a "love of country" which implies a directly social solidarity.

the prestige of self-importance, as expressed through superiority over others attested by conquest, seems to carry Veblen far away from an economic interpretation of history. But it hardly places him in accord with what may be termed the orthodox view of patriotism. For though that view gives a not unimportant place to war, it is a reputedly defensive war that is approved, rather a war for one's country than a war of conquest. The nationalism identified with patriotism is not generally understood, as aggressive, expansive, imperialistic, though it may develop these tendencies. To Veblen, however, these qualities are of the essence of patriotism which is the modern form taken by the predatory, invidious, contentious element in the animal man. The interested feeling of a nation towards others, however, carries two opposed economic and social tendencies. One is to have as little to do with them as possible, either in the way of personal contacts or of trade, a policy of isolation. The nationalist ferment, left everywhere by the Great War, finds a striking illustration of this tendency in the tariffs, embargoes, subsidies and other devices for reducing to a minimum the economic and personal relations between the different countries. Though complete economic isolation is not possible for any people, the extent of such dependency on foreign supplies can be greatly reduced, and bans can be placed upon the entrance or residence of foreigners in "our" country. This policy might seem at first sight to make for peace and for a merely inclusive "patriotism." But such a solution could not satisfy Veblen's view of the patriotic animus which requires conflict with a view to conquest. The isolationist policy is, therefore, accompanied by its opposite, an imperialism which is, primarily, an assertion of superior power expressed in territorial enlargement, secondarily, a seizure of the national resources and markets of backward countries. The Boer War he cites as a plain modern instance of this co-operation of sentimental imperialism and business enterprise. Indeed, this conjunction was strikingly personified in the character and career of Cecil Rhodes. But Veblen was writing during the Great War and his mind was naturally concentrated on "Imperial Germany" as the purposive war-maker. His analysis of this imperial animus, however, relates the political urge closely to the economic conditions. "What makes the German Imperial establishment redoubtable, beyond comparison, is the very simple but also very grave combination of circumstances whereby the German people have acquired the use of the modern industrial arts in the highest state of efficiency, at the same time that they have retained unabated the fanatical loyalty of feudal barbarism. So long, and in so far, as this conjunction of forces holds, there is no out-look for peace except in the elimination of Germany, as a power capable of disturbing the peace."[1]

The decay of this dynastic spirit, in Germany or elsewhere, appeared to Veblen a slow and dubious affair. He saw very clearly the impetus given to militant nationalism by the War. "As a preliminary consideration, those peoples of the Empire and its allies, as well as their enemies in the Great War, will necessarily come out of this war-like experience in a more patriotic and more vindictive frame of mind than that in which they entered on this adventure. Fighting makes for malevolence."[2]

Against this array of irrational emotionalism, reason and calculated self-interest do not avail. The manifest advantage to all nations of free commerce and co-operative enterprise in opening up the full resources of the globe, the gains and amenities of equal access to all countries for travellers and settlers, the full use of the new powers of communications making for a common standard of civilization, not merely fail to convince the national patriot, they are even treated as dangerous invasions of his collective and

[1] *The Nature of Peace*, p. 202.   [2] Op. cit., p. 195.

individual personality. No more powerful testimony to this temper is possible than the cultivation, nay the worship, of their separate language which small nations maintain as barriers to free communication with outsiders.

Though Veblen, as we see, finds the main source of international conflict in a patriotism that is not primarily economic in its origin and aim, he clearly recognizes that the conservatism of class-distinctions and discipline which patriotism in its militant aspect inculcates is of great assistance in stopping class-war and in preserving the rights of the possessing class within such patriotic nations. It is not merely the half-conscious cunning which the rulers employ, when trouble brews at home, to "stay giddy minds with foreign quarrels." It is also the persistent popular superstition which holds that a successful war, with conquest and dictated terms of peace can be profitable, not merely to particular capitalist or financial interests but in some mysterious manner to "the people" that bears the cost of war in lives and money. Veblen roundly asserts that "the preservation of the present pecuniary law and order, with all its incidents of ownership and investment, is incompatible with an unwar-like state of peace and security."[1] For a reliable peaceful world,

[1] Op. cit., p. 316.

from which the waste of war and armaments were eliminated, and where free mobility and trade led each people to use its productive resources most advantageously, would bring either an organized international sabotage by the owning classes, or such radical reforms in the distribution of wealth as would everywhere introduce an economic and social equalitarianism which has always been regarded as vain Utopianism. Veblen evidently thinks the former alternative more likely to occur as a result of attempts at international pacification after the Great War. For pacific internationalism, which leaves the capitalist control within each country intact, would promote international contests for the control of world-markets in raw materials and other key products, and would evoke an inter-imperialist policy in the profitable development of China and other backward countries. Though Veblen does not directly discuss the effect of such a policy in mitigating national sabotage by finding large foreign outlets for otherwise surplus products, it lies within the scope of his financial theory and forms a manifest alternative to the economic conflicts between capitalist groups which hitherto have pressed their profitable interests upon their national governments.

Though the League of Nations had not come

THE FIELD OF POLITICS

into existence when Veblen wrote on "The Nature of Peace" it was under contemplation as a likely outcome of peace-terms, and he has some interesting comments to make upon its possibilities. Though other than distinctively economic interests incite to war, the war temper being an expression of the whole psychical contents of inflamed nationalism, a settled peace can never be obtained except upon a reasonable and equitable arrangement which will give all peoples free access to world markets and rights of settlement. A League of Nations, in which each nation strives to keep its own markets for its own producers by tariffs, embargoes, and other barriers, while it endeavours to obtain political and economic control of the raw materials and markets of backward countries as colonies, protectorates or "spheres of influence" must fail to keep the peace. The first condition for a settled peace by international agreement must be what Veblen terms the "neutralization" of "the material and commercial interests of the federated peoples."[1] In other words, the abandonment of a colonial or imperial policy, operated in the economic interests of any power, is essential to peace. Under neutralization, as here conceived, colonies would cease to be "colonial possessions" in the predatory sense.

[1] Op. cit., p. 258.

Though Veblen clearly recognizes the advantages of the neutral policy here adumbrated to all members of the League in terms alike of peace and wealth, he also recognizes the opposition likely to occur from the imperialistic attitude of Germany. "In the Imperial colonial policy colonies are conceived to stand to their Imperial guardian or master in a relation between that of a step-child and that of an indentured servant; to be dealt with summarily and at discretion and to be made use of without scruple."[1] The disposition to become a "self-sufficing economic whole" he attributes to the survival of the dynastic instinct, holding that all restraints of trade between nations weaken and impoverish them economically. The dynastic instinct has however two supports, the pride of self-sufficiency and its utility in the event of war. What Veblen could not perceive was the two related obstacles to effective peace which would confront the League after the war was over and the bad peace was in operation. The first was the failure of the several League nations to realize and to insure the gainful policy of free-trade and the general tendency towards an attitude of economic isolation. This might have been predicted by one so impressed, as Veblen was, by the increasing pace of technological productivity

[1] Op. cit., p. 261.

in the industrial arts of all capitalist countries, had he applied his theory of pecuniary control to other countries than America. For the protective policy of limited world-trade adopted by all capitalist countries is manifestly due to the existence within each country of productive power that is excessive in the sense that the goods it could produce are withheld because they could not find a profitable market either at home or abroad. How far this general phenomenon is rightly explained by Veblen's theory of "sabotage" may indeed be questioned. But it might have been expected that he would have foreseen this economic check upon League efficiency. The second obstacle to effective pacificism, the rising hostility between the "haves" and the "have nots" in the sense of colonial possessors, could not, of course, have arisen, if the prime condition of "neutralization" had been fulfilled. For, dynastic animus apart, no country would seek colonial empire if all backward countries were freely accessible to its trade and surplus population. Veblen realizes clearly the difficulties which the cause of peace will encounter from the certainty that the early proceedings of a League must be conducted in an atmosphere of inflamed nationalism and that the representatives of the constituent nations will be members or nominees of the owning classes in each nation, so that patriotism, both in its political and its economic implications, will restrict the possibilities of a genuinely international policy. Indeed, he does not conceal his suspicions that the League may be utilized to repress any really dangerous class-action within one of its member states.

"Should difficulties then arise between those who own and those who do not, it would become a nice question whether the compact to preserve the power and national integrity of the several nations comprised in the League should be held to cover the case of internal dissensions and possible disorders partaking of the nature of revolt against the established authorities or against the established provisions of law. It is always conceivable that a national government standing on a somewhat conservative maintenance of the received law and order might feel itself bound by its conception of the peace to make common cause with the keepers of established rights in neighbouring states, particularly if the similar interests of their own nation were thought to be placed in jeopardy by the course of events."[1]

Veblen's profound conviction of the emotional force and the complete irrationality of patriotism and nationalism apparently disable him from

[1] Op. cit., pp. 318–9.

any sincere belief in the possibility of an effective world-government which would accord with his own feelings and beliefs. He would doubtless have liked to believe in an extension of his ideal of a technician's economic government within each nation to the wider international field. But the two obstacles of patriotism and pecuniary power render such a policy unattainable. Veblen does indeed envisage the probability that a settled peace might bring "a curtailment or abrogation" of some of the rights of ownership and disposal of property, especially in the form of investments, presumably under the pressure or fear of mass revolution in the several advanced industrial countries. But he is, perhaps purposely, so obscure in his statement of this "probability" as to reduce it to the level of a remote possibility. "Not much can confidently be said as to the details of such a prospective revision of legal rights but the analogy of that procedure by which these other vested rights (i.e., of feudalism and the dynastic monarchy) have been reduced to a manageable disability, suggests that the method in the present case also would be by way of curtailment, abrogation and elimination."[1]

But though he throws out this probability, or possibility, of a progressive displacement of the

[1] Op. cit., p. 329.

current "price system" in the hands of financial profiteers, he ends his speculation upon the line of an interpretation more congenial to his central economic thesis, the combined dominion of pecuniary power and patriotism. Should peace be established on an international basis, it might have appeared reasonable to assume that national economy would gradually but effectively be displaced by a world-economy in which the resources and the markets of the world would be placed at the free and equal disposal of the business men of all countries. In fact such an implication would appear to be a necessary requisite for a peaceful world. Such a world-economy would seem to demand an extension of the finance of international cartels and similar business arrangements for sharing markets, regulating prices and securing profits. But Veblen does not appear to contemplate any abatement of the economic nationalism which enables financiers to sabotage the home market. If peace be established "The new dispensation offers two new factors bearing on this business-like need of a sagacious sabotage, or rather it brings a change of coefficients in two factors already familiar in business management: a greater need, for gainful business, of resorting to such limitation of traffic; and a greater facility of ways and means for enforcing the needed restrictions"—"The outcome to be looked for should apparently be such an effectual recourse to capitalistic sabotage as will neutralize any added advantage that might otherwise accrue to the community from its continued improvement in technology."[1] There is nothing to indicate that by "the community" he signifies anything but the nation, or that he contemplates any capitalistic sabotage on an international scale. Though this position is in keeping with his refusal to recognize the limits set upon his profitable policy of sabotage by the possibility of expansive foreign markets, it is very strange that he should ignore the dependence of "the peace" which he contemplates upon some form, whether capitalistic or socialistic, of economic internationalism.

But his eyes seem set upon a distinctively national economy for America in which "The logical result should be an accelerated rate of accumulation of the country's wealth in the hands of a relatively very small class of wealthy owners, with a relatively inconsiderable semi-dependent middle class of the well-to-do, and with the mass of the population even more nearly destitute than they are to-day."[2]

Had he been taxed with the neglect of economic internationalism, probably he would have replied

[1] Op. cit., p. 341.   [2] Op. cit., p. 344.

that he was concerned with the early implications of a settled peace, and that the achievement of any effective international economy, either of a capitalist or a socialist order, lay in a distant future, and demanded the slow process of the decay of "the nationalist animus."

"The motives that work out through this national spirit, by use of this patriotic order, fall under two heads: dynastic ambition and business enterprise. The two categories have the common trait that neither the one nor the other comprises anything that is of the slightest benefit to the community at large; but both have at the same time a high prestige value in the conventional esteem of modern men."[1] In other words, we are dealing with archaic notions and valuations which cannot be eradicated by a direct appeal to reason or intelligent self-interest. For the gradual decay of patriotic nationalism, as of other prestigious and magical superstitions Veblen looks mainly to the education of the common man under the regime of modern mechanical arts. "The man who is so held by his daily employment and his life-long attention within the range of habits of thought that are valid in the mechanistic technology, will, on the average and in the long run, lose his grip upon the spiritual virtues of

[1] Op. cit., p. 284.

THE FIELD OF POLITICS

national prestige and dynastic primacy; 'for they are foolishness unto him; neither can he know them, because they are spiritually discerned.'" So "with the passage of time pervasively by imperceptible displacement, by the decay of habitual disuse, as well as by habitual occupation with these other and unrelated ways and means of knowledge and belief, dynastic loyalty and the like conceptions in the realm of religion and magic pass out of the field of attention and fall insensibly into the category of the lost arts."[1]

In the final pages of his *Nature of Peace* Veblen shows how the moulding logic of mechanical technology must weaken the supports which property and ownership receive from other than political and economic sources. Two such supports are the religious beliefs, with the institutions in which they are incorporated, and the respect for law. Now both these supports are undermined and weakened by the new mechanistic habits of life and thought. The support rendered by religion to the conservation of the political-economic system takes two forms. First comes the diversion of the popular mind from the defects and sufferings of this world to the compensations of a better world to come. To describe religion as a conscious policy of "dope" is, no doubt, a

[1] Op. cit., pp. 198-9.

shallow criticism. Nor does history always bear out the suggestion that the consolations of religion necessarily weaken the demand for reforms of man's condition of life in this world. Not only do religious movements such as that of the Anabaptists, and the Independents in the Puritan revolution, carry direct demands for justice in political and economic arrangements, but the whole spirit of Protestantism, with its denial of religious authoritarianism and its congregational co-operation, encourages an attitude of criticism in the general outlook of its adherents. For religion cannot be kept as a watertight compartment in human mentality. So far as freedom of thought is allowed to enter the religious field, it is certain to stray into adjoining fields of thought and action. But with due allowance for this consideration, it remains true that the absorption of religion in the preparations for another world together with the conception of that world in terms of autocratic government and vacuous happiness, have necessarily operated to draw men's minds away from close scrutiny and passionate revolt against this world's injustice and oppression. What after all are three score years and ten compared with eternity? The rather rapid fading of religious beliefs and church adhesions that has been taking place in most Western nations during this genera-

THE FIELD OF POLITICS

tion is not, of course, attributable wholly to the modernist turn of mind which Veblen stresses. Even the meagre form of popular education which has reached the masses has helped to arouse a critical attitude towards the supernatural and towards the political and economic rule of the wealthy classes. So the potent conservatism which the Churches exercised for the preservation of the established order, with its divinely appointed class status, has largely disappeared, leaving the people with no firm belief in another world, and a proportionately stronger disposition to endeavour to "make the best" of this world.

But it would be idle to ignore the more direct support to "property" and ownership which the Churches have given in virtue of the accumulation of wealth which has come to them, partly by the voluntary liberality of the rich, partly by the skilled business arts exercised by them in the exchange of other world's goods for this world's goods. The practices of the Catholic Church throughout the Middle Ages, in the sale of pardons and indulgences and in death-bed pressures on the penitent rich, are only extreme and blatant cases of an art far more subtle and persistent in its economic yield. But though the possession and management of wealth acquired in the past involve a sympathetic acceptance of current business practices which supports a conservative temper and attitude of mind in the Church authorities, far more important is the dependence of many of these institutions upon the current liberality of wealthy members. How is it possible to expect from the dependent clergy of such churches a wide sympathy towards efforts to reform an economic order when riches come from the ownership of land and the profitable employment of labour?

This, however, was not the aspect of religion which most appealed to Veblen, nor does he in any of his writings give it the amount of attention it deserves. He regards the Churches as institutions for the exhibition of vicarious leisure and conspicuous waste, or, in other words, as outlets of the predaceous instinct in its pecuniary aspect. This at any rate is the attitude adopted in his *Theory of the Leisure Class*. Large expenditure is associated with little physical convenience or comfort to the congregation. "In the most reputable latter-day houses of worship, where no expense is spared, the principle of austerity is carried to the length of making the fittings of the place a means of mortifying the flesh, especially in appearance.—This canon of devout austerity is based on the pecuniary reputability of conspicuously wasteful consumption, backed by the principle that vicarious consumption should conspicuously not conduce to the comfort of the vicarious consumer."[1] As with the building, so with the service. "The rehearsal of the service (the term 'service' carries a suggestive significance for the point in question) grows more perfunctory as the cult gains in age and consistency, and this perfunctoriness is very pleasing to the correct devout taste. And with a good reason, for the fact of its being perfunctory goes to say pointedly that the master for whom it is performed is exalted above the vulgar need of actually proficient service on the part of his servants. They are unprofitable servants, and there is an honorific implication for their master in their remaining unprofitable."[2]

But in his later writings Veblen makes it clear that the mentality, superstitious and ascetic, which has found expression in this order of extravagant expenditure, is being sapped by the restrictions of a mechanical working life.

"It should not be difficult to conceive the general course of such a decay of superstitions under the unremitting discipline of mechanistic habits of life. The recent past offers an illustration in the unemotional progress of decay that has overtaken religious beliefs in the more civilized countries; and more particularly among the

[1] *Theory of the Leisure Class*, p. 121. [2] Op. cit., p. 123.

intellectually trained workmen of the mechanical industries. The elimination of such non-mechanistic propositions of the faith has been visibly going on, but it has not worked out on any uniform plan, nor has it overtaken any large or compact body of people consistently or abruptly, being of the nature of obsolescence rather than of set repudiation. But in a slack and more fleeting fashion the divestment has gone on until the aggregate result is unmistakable."[1]

The decline of religious beliefs gives increased importance to the popular respect for secular laws as a safeguard of property and ownership. Veblen finds that the now visible abuses of the current rights of property under the pecuniary system of control which dissociates ownership from any visible productive effort arouses a growing dissatisfaction with legal processes among the conscious sections of the working classes. Legal systems in their relation to industry and property are necessarily rooted in conditions that are obsolete in a changing world. But it is natural that modern attempts to place rights of property upon a basis more equitable and reasonable, and more conducive to general welfare, should be met by the firm use of legal resistance on the part of owners whose "rights" are threatened.

[1] *The Nature of Peace*, p. 363.

THE FIELD OF POLITICS

The difficulties encountered even in democratic countries by movements to reform the law and its administration are so grave as to tempt the workers into definitely revolutionary action. The profession of the law is itself a powerful pecuniary interest linked by bonds of sympathy with the rights of ownership which it is its province to defend. In America perhaps more than in Europe the law, however loose in its defence of life and liberty, is tight in its defence of the constitutional and legal rights of property. For a written constitution, ill adapted to the economic requirements of to-day, but hedged round with barriers to amendment, forms the strongest citadel of defence for the owning and profiteering classes. Recent events bring into dramatic relief the impending struggle between the democratic principle as expressed in measures of the New Deal and the obsolescent Constitution. The issue is not a simple one from the standpoint of American mentality. For there is a powerful force of superstitious sentimentality in respectable Americans which refuses to touch the sacred Constitution with impious hands. At the same time its rigid defence of the rights of a rich and ruling few shocks the minds of those who recognize the requirements of a changing economic world. Veblen views the coming situation with grave concern. "So soon, or rather so far, as the common man comes to realize that those rights of ownership and investment uniformly work to his material detriment, at the same time that he has lost the 'will to believe' in any argument that does not run in terms of the mechanistic logic, it is reasonable to expect that he will take a stand on this matter: and it is more than likely that the stand taken will be of an uncompromising kind—presumably something of the stand once taken by recalcitrant Englishmen in protest against the irresponsible rule of the Stuart sovereigns. It is also not likely that the beneficiaries under these proprietary rights will yield their ground at all amicably: all the more since they are patently within their authentic rights in insisting on full discretion in the disposal of their own possessions." —"And as happens when two antagonistic parties are each convinced of the justice of its cause, and in the absence of an umpire, the logical recourse is the wager of battle."[1]

But though history teaches that in such situations a recourse to the arbitrament of force takes place, it likewise teaches the enormous "damage, discomfort and shame" attendant on such use of force. It, therefore, remains possible that the cruder logic may be tempered by a wiser

[1] Op. cit., p. 365.

discretion on the part of the owners, who may be disposed to make such concessions as will enable them to continue their economic rule in a modified form, abating and perhaps in the long run abrogating "the rights of property and of the price-system in which these rights take effect."[1] On this cautious note of hope Veblen ends his thesis. It is evident that in Western Europe, governmental action or working-class action, or voluntary conduct in ownership and control of industry, or all these factors in various degrees of co-operation, are securing important modifications of the rights of ownership and the related distribution of wealth. Post-War popular movements along socialist lines in several countries, and in particular the success of the Soviet revolution in Russia, have undoubtedly reinforced the concessionary movements in the more democratic nations. Whether the stiffer individualism of the possessing class in America, supported by a Constitution, a Party system, and an administrative and judicial system which has always been their servant, will recognize the desirability of a socialistic policy of concession and reformation as the alternative to a class-struggle of violence with uncertain victory, remains one of the greatest unsettled questions of our age.

[1] Op. cit., p. 367.

CHAPTER VIII

PERSONAL PRESTIGE

PERHAPS the most interesting and original section of Veblen's sociology lies outside the fields of economics, politics and religion and consists of excursions into the less-organized social habits and activities in which the predatory spirit, co-operating with and modified by other human instincts or dispositions, finds expression. For there are many activities which interest most men more than industry, politics and religion. Games and sports, prestigious displays of various kinds in personal demeanour, language and deportment, in the utilization of one's family and dependants for vicarious leisure and conspicuous waste, the parade of dress and the ritual of social duties—these play a really important part as derivations and sublimations of the predaceous instinct which finds its chief modern expression in pecuniary strength.

These social activities in which the modern man can express his excellence can only be rightly understood when they are related to archaic habits of self-display or emulation. "Conspicuous waste and conspicuous leisure are reputable because they are evidence of pecuniary strength; pecuniary strength is reputable or honorific because, in the last analysis, it argues success and superior force." So we may expect to find in the social life of the owning classes of our time the artificially elaborated remnants of original barbarian tastes. The best gateway to this subject is the word "virtue." In its early meaning the quality denoted by this word is without question physical force, the fighting power, upon which a man chiefly "prides" himself and measures his superiority over his fellows. We need not, however, assume that man in his primitive condition is a fighting animal, with a preference for conquest over his fellows and a distaste for work. On the contrary Veblen expresses the view that the earliest man was a pacific creature, a social being in his group and moved by a spirit of workmanship for the attainment of his food and other requisites of survival. It is only when the limits of physical environment drive him into predaceous practices that hunting and fighting become his distinctive occupations, and that a life of violent exploit separates him from peaceful productive activities which are delegated to women and serfs and lose for him the "interest" which nature attaches to all serviceable activities.[1] When the simpler forms of fighting are repressed in ordinary life by civilization, attachment to the fighting services of our country continues to be the most honourable occupation, for countless ages the only profession worthy of a gentleman. Though the conditions of modern warfare (save in the air) do not offer the earlier opportunities for personal exploit and the "science" of war calls for some qualities of brain not in close keeping with the cruder fighting powers, military service still remains honorific for those in command, though conscription has everywhere diminished the prestige for the rank and file. The ready popular response to an authoritative appeal for the defence of our country is due, not chiefly to any sense of duty, but to a sudden reawakening of the primitive fighting instinct.

The survival of this combative instinct for most men in peace-time, however, takes shape in the zeal for sports and games. Boxing and bull-fighting are, of course, the simplest examples of the personal practice and the spectatorial interest in this type of virtue. There are few men who would not in their secret hearts prefer to possess

[1] This topic, already handled in his *Leisure Class*, Veblen treats more fully in his volume *The Instinct of Workmanship*—a development of his essay on the same topic published in the American *Journal of Sociology*, September, 1898.

the ability of a Carnera to fell any enemy with his fist to any higher form of ability, though they might deny this preference and even believe in their denial. For such denial is the tribute which barbarism pays to civilization. But more intricate and far more interesting are the sublimations of the fighting instinct which pervade the sports wherein prestige may be acquired. And here we encounter other interests interwoven with pugnacity. The play of man, as of other animals, has notoriously a survival value as the imaginative practice of a skill useful for food-getting and other purposes, though the struggle against other animals is seldom absent as a stimulus. This play has a zest attached to it ultimately derived from the biological utility it serves. It is this zest that furnishes the animus, the interest and excitement, attaching to what in distinction from pure "play" we call games and sports. Some sports, such as hunting and shooting, are reputable because they are traditional survivals of the serviceable pursuits of earlier ages of man. The social prestige attaching to them is, no doubt, partly derived from the skill and courage attested by success, but is mainly derived from the traditional connexions with the life of a landed aristocracy. The Master of the Hunt is a title of high personal honour. The early catching and killing of animals was a productive employment. But "sport" must separate itself from this utilitarian purpose. "As the community passes out of the hunting stage proper, hunting gradually becomes differentiated into two distinct employments. On the one hand it is a trade, carried on chiefly for gain; and from this the element of exploit is virtually absent.—On the other hand, the chase is also a sport—an exercise of the predatory impulse simply. As such it does not afford any appreciable pecuniary incentive, but it contains a more or less obvious element of exploit."[1] His summary of the situation is best rendered in a later passage of his *Leisure Class*. "Sports of all kinds are of the same general character, including prize fights, bull fights, athletics, shooting, angling, yachting and games of skill, even where the element of destructive physical efficiency is not an obtrusive feature. Sports shade off from the basis of hostile combat, through skill to cunning and chicanery, without its being possible to draw the line at any point."[2]

An integral factor in "exploit" is risk-taking. This may signify the exposure of one's person to danger, as in such games as football or big-game hunting. Or it may take an economic form, as in the betting that has come to play the widest

[1] *Leisure Class*, p. 41. [2] Op. cit., p. 255.

PERSONAL PRESTIGE

part in most modern sports which may be rated in three grades, the actors, the spectators, the gamblers. The psychology of gambling and the rapid spread of the vogue in recent times is not difficult to explain. There are several contributory causes. It is commonly attributed to the desire for relief from the boredom of a routine life which, on its work side and its leisure side, offers too little opportunity for the spirit of adventure. Life has for most people become too mechanical in its detail, too certain in its causation. No doubt it contains large elements of insecurity for most of us, but they mostly lie outside our conscious handling. Gambling and games of chance, therefore, appeal to our pleasure in surprise. They consciously combine some pride in skilled prediction with the interest in the unpredictable. This goes right back into the primitive magic of the savage whose animism enables him to believe that by some more or less skilled ritual he can affect events that lie outside his ordinary sphere of control. The survival of this superstitious attitude is, of course, illustrated in the various avoidances, such as spilling salt, sitting thirteen at table, looking at the new moon through a glass, as well as in the more positive faith in charms and mascots as serviceable instruments of protection. Plenty of "educated" persons believe in "systems" applied to the roulette-table at Monte Carlo, by which luck may be converted into some rational order that will enable them to win. Most persons, if you put it to them suddenly, will admit that in *rouge et noir*, if they come into the game when red had turned up twelve times consecutively, they would bet in favour of black for the next pull, although upon reflection they would see the fallacy of supposing that the chance of any one pull was affected by what went before. The general belief in luck is doubtless supported by dramatic instances of persons who have "made good" without exhibiting any obvious merits. But it has a deeper and a more intelligible support from the fact that the causation of the great majority of minor deeds and happenings is not discernible. In dressing, eating and other incidents of ordinary life, routine, almost automatic, is accompanied by trifling departures from routine, slight changes in the order, the reason for which we cannot detect. Sometimes we butter the toast before pouring out the tea, or put in the sugar before putting in the milk, and so on. These trifling variations may be a subconscious kick against routine, but they carry the appearance of chance. And they are so pervasive as to support the belief, to which even important scientists now commit themselves, that "chance" is a real

PERSONAL PRESTIGE

determining factor in physical events and in human conduct. Though most thinkers still retain the conviction that chance means nothing else than ignorance of cause, the expulsion of cause itself from scientific procedure will serve to uphold the human interest which undoubtedly continues to adhere to the unpredictable.

In analysing sport and gambling it is, therefore, easy to realize the human appeal which the combination of prowess and chance make to people. When the improvement of the common lot has given a public education which enables everyone to read the "tips" and calculate the "odds," while most people find themselves in possession of some slight pecuniary margin beyond the necessaries of life, we can easily understand how the gambling habit has become at once an alleviation of routine and an imitative copy of the prestigious practices of "our betters."

Sport, though primarily based on personal exploit and prestige does not rest there. It is carried forward into the various social groupings, becoming an important element in local and national patriotism. Every town and village with its cricket and football club, every school and university with its athletic apparatus, seeks collective kudos from each form of competitive sport.

The chief British-American contribution to

modern world civilization is the extension of this sports animus. Indeed, it has occurred to some psychologists that the abolition of international war may possibly be achieved, not by the moral appeal to peace, or the rational appeal to sound commercial interests, but by a sublimation of the crude fighting instinct into contests and victories in games, an extension into the broad international field of the play-conflicts which has displaced the ruder conflicts which prevailed in each country before the achievement of national law and order.

Sport, however, is only one of the social ways in which the craving for prestige, personal or class, finds expression. Some of Veblen's most interesting researches are into the private practices by which the pecuniary *élite* express their self-importance in conspicuous waste and leisure, copied so far as means permit by the middle and lower classes.

What Veblen calls "the pecuniary canons of taste" carry us from sport to the domestic animals whose ownership, breeding and training have a prestigious value. Dogs and horses fall into the category, in so far as they perform no useful service and are valued for sporting or for purely honorific purposes. "The dog commends himself to our favour by affording play to our propensity for mastery, and as he is also an item of expense, and commonly serves no industrial purpose, he holds an assured place in man's regard as a thing of good repute. The dog is at the same time associated in our imagination with the chase—a meritorious employment and an expression of the honourable predatory impulse."[1] In pursuance of this role the dog is subjected to variations of breeding which are designed to produce deformities. "The animal value of curious monstrosities, such as the prevailing styles of pet dogs both for men's and women's use, rests on this high cost of production, and their value to their owners lies chiefly in their utility as items of conspicuous consumption."[2] It is interesting to note how easily æsthetic values of beauty and fitness accommodate themselves to such departures from nature and find pleasure in rare shapes of ugliness and deformity.

The horse stands in a slightly different position. His economic utility for transport is disappearing fast under the competition of motor traffic. It might seem as if the motor-car was destined to supersede the horse even for pleasure-riding. This would have happened if the possession and use of motor-cars had remained a rich man's privilege, as it was a generation ago. But the

[1] Op. cit., p. 141.   [2] Op. cit., p. 142.

descent of the motor-car into general use for all sorts and conditions of men ruined this early prestigious value, which now only survives in part as attached to a few obviously expensive makes. This has brought about a conscious survival and revival of riding as a prestigious protest against the social degradation of the car. The best people ride more than formerly, and hunting as a sport has gained in vogue. Thus the horse, displaced almost entirely from utility, has acquired a new rarity value as an emblem of "class" dignity. This, of course, has affected horse breeding, for the modern horse is bred for speed and grace, for actual or potential success in racing, which still remains the most prestigious of all sports for the rich man and the gambling public.

We have already touched upon the term virtue in its proper significance of manliness. But hardly less significant is the use it still bears when applied to women, viz., chastity. For this meaning implies that woman, for wifehood, is man's exclusive possession for sexual purposes. The virtuous wife must be the authenticated mother of his children to help him transmit and perpetuate his family prestige and property. In earlier times this wife and mother ruled the affairs of the home for him while he spent his time and energies in more

PERSONAL PRESTIGE

directly prestigious exploits. To such home work she would add the duller or more routine labour of agriculture or of superintending these sorts of labour as performed by serfs. Not until comparatively modern times did pecuniary circumstances equip her for the full life of a "lady" in conspicuous waste and leisure. Indeed this is never completely attainable. For though she should not "soil her hands" with any menial work, and may even delegate to a paid housekeeper the supervision of such work, the social duties devolving on her and the effective practice of ostentatious expenditure may leave her little leisure in the sense of idle time. This applies not merely to the rich but to large sections of middle-class women sufficiently well off to employ domestic service and with few or no children to "look after." Indeed the practice of birth control and the habit of putting quite young children into boarding-schools liberate a large proportion of fairly well-to-do mothers for "social duties" and personal enjoyments which may fully occupy their time in prestigious ways.[1]

What arms are to the man as fighting animal,

---

[1] Veblen, I think, fails to note the special value of the dog (to a less degree the cat) as a child-substitute to women. The care bestowed on dogs to keep them clean (Veblen notes their filthy habits which apparently do not disgust the most refined women) and properly fed and exercised, is manifestly of the nature of an *ersatz*.

dress is to the woman for sex rivalry and conspicuous consumption. In his discussion of Dress as an expression of the Pecuniary Culture Veblen sets forth the distinctive qualities of reputable clothing both for men and woman. In both cases dress should be expensive and should plainly indicate that the wearer is not engaged in any sort of productive labour.

Neat and spotless clothing for a man indicate that he cannot perform any sort of manual labour. A century ago the typical English gentleman wore richly coloured and decorative suits unfitted for the performance even of professional or commercial work. Though plenty of the scions of aristocratic families were going into the city, or otherwise busying themselves with money-making pursuits, the old standards of dress were maintained until their obvious inconvenience brought nineteenth century displacement in favour of the plain frock-coats and high hats, which are now in their turn passing into desuetude. Indeed, for men, dress is becoming ever a less effective assertion of wealth and prestige, since the higher income level of the "lower classes" and the growth of mass-production enable them to wear specious imitations of the more costly garments of the well-to-do. This applies to the dress of women as much as to that of men for most social purposes, though not for all. Veblen in several of his writings makes a close scrutiny of woman's dress in its social significance. An early essay (1894) upon the "Economic Theory of Women's Dress" is published in the posthumous volume of his writings, entitled *Essays in our Changing Order* (The Viking Press, 1934) appropriately following a somewhat later article upon "The Barbarian Status of Women" (1899). There he distinguishes the two origins of dress for physical protection and comfort, on the one hand, for ornament upon the other. Sometimes these two purposes converge or even coincide, sometimes they are incompatible and preference then is generally given to the purpose of ornament, which both for males and females is accepted as the prime origin of apparel. These earliest uses were not, however, strictly economic, in Veblen's sense, i.e., as an index of the wealth of the owner, or, as in the case of woman, the owner's owner. It was not until the patriarchal organization of society was established that women's dress became "an exponent of the wealth of the men whose chattels they were."[1]

From these patriarchal times up to the present women's ornaments have not, of course, been confined to their apparel, but have included

[1] *Essays in our Changing Order*, p. 67.

bracelets, anklets, rings and other tokens of conspicuously useless or even burdensome expenditure. Veblen here and elsewhere examines the subsidiary part in this "economy" played by milliners and fashion-makers who exploit the novelty needed to give distinction to a wearer when the former adornments have become too "common."

Conspicuous expenditure operates in two ways, first, to exhibit the pecuniary power and prestige of the owner, secondly, to indicate the idleness of the woman-wearer. For this latter purpose some articles of dress should be positively detrimental to physical activity, as in the case of the long skirt or the high heels. "The corset is, in economic theory, substantially a mutilation, undergone for the purpose of lowering the subject's vitality and rendering her permanently and obviously unfit for work. It is true, the corset impairs the personal attraction of the woman, but the loss sustained on that score is offset by the gain in reputability which comes of her visibly increased expensiveness and infirmity."[1]

The corset and the long skirt have almost disappeared, chiefly owing to women's increased interest in active sports where it is obviously too detrimental. But in general dress fashions move more restlessly than ever and are followed

[1] *Leisure Class*, p. 172.

more quickly by an increasing proportion of the sex. Veblen attempts to explain the phenomenon as inherent in the process of adornment when pecuniary display is confronted with a natural search after beauty. "The changing styles are the expression of a restless search for something which shall commend itself to our æsthetic sense; but as each innovation is subject to the selective action of the norm of conspicuous waste, the range within which innovation can take place is somewhat restricted. The innovation must not only be more beautiful, or perhaps oftener, less offensive, than that which it displaces, but it must also come up to the accepted standard of expensiveness."[1] Mere novelty arouses the interest both of the wearer and the spectator and is an obvious mode of self-assertion. So far as it becomes the fashion for a limited reputable class, it is felt to be beautiful. But this shallow sense of beauty quickly evaporates with time and imitation by the less reputable classes. Veblen holds that a genuinely æsthetic taste which secretly causes satisfaction produces a restiveness with fashions whose chief or only attraction lies in their novelty and expense. But dress as a mode of conspicuous waste need not be novel. It may be archaic as is the case of certain domestic servants of the lackey class,

[1] Op. cit., p. 174.

designed to suggest long-established family importance on the part of their employers. This archaic character is also represented, in accentuated form, in priestly raiment when "the vestments, properly so called, are ornate, grotesque, inconvenient and, at least ostensibly, comfortless to the point of distress."[1]

. . . . .

Apart from the comparatively superficial changes which either fashion or technological advance effects upon the prestigious display of the well-to-do classes, there remains in the deeper strata of their thought and valuations a firm conservatism. Though in the last resort this mentality may be traced to the subconscious defence of property, the crude assertion of this economic determinism will not satisfy most thinkers. This conservatism is by no means confined to the field of economics and politics, nor does it rest on any merely selfish calculation of personal advantages. "It is an instinctive revulsion at any departure from the accepted way of doing and looking at things—a revulsion common to all men and only to be overcome by stress of circumstances"—"The members of the wealthy class do not yield to the demand for innovation as readily as other man because they are not constrained to do so."[2]

[1] Op. cit., p. 183. [2] Op. cit., p. 199.

PERSONAL PRESTIGE

Respectability and "good form" are social instruments of this conservatism, and, as their standards are set by persons of wealth and high position, they have an immense influence upon the less wealthy classes, especially in countries like America and Britain where class distinctions are not so rigid that each class forms its own conventions and traditions. When social-economic climbing is not too rare and difficult, the habits and valuations of the middle, and to a less extent the working classes are moulded by half-conscious imitation upon upper-class standards. This snobbish admiration of one's "betters" is, of course, chiefly conspicuous in the abler and more adventurous persons who have an opportunity to rise into a higher social-economic grade. But the more torpid mind of the mass is infected with a conservatism, which is hardly less pronounced, though of a somewhat different origin. In Britain, though to a less degree in America, the mass of the people has a rooted aversion from the free energetic exercise of their mind, and when their "natural" leaders and teachers are taken from them by accessibility to higher states, they lie in a mental condition that is not easily receptive of disturbing thoughts or responsive to revolutionary appeals. That innovations of considerable importance can take place history testifies, but they generally occur in periods when war or other concrete disturbance has seriously upset the whole national fabric. Veblen lays his finger upon the chief obstacle to reforms when he stresses the organic interdependence of all social institutions. For it is almost inevitable that reform processes should begin with the redress of certain urgent grievances and proceed along a path of gradualness. But "The code of preparation, conventionalities and usages in vogue at any given time and among any given people has more or less the character of an organic whole, so that any appreciable change in one point of the scheme involves something of a change or readjustment at other points also, if not a reorganization all along the line." Except in an atmosphere of revolution it is difficult or impossible to get "the people" to attempt action upon this plane. Their latent conservatism inhibits such strenuous activity and such gigantic risk-taking. A perception of this popular mentality favours attempts to establish great national reforms by the will of ministers, usurping or stampeding the consent of the people.

CHAPTER IX

A SUMMARY AND ESTIMATE

THE importance of Veblen's wider contribution to sociology has been somewhat obscured by the dramatic prominence given to his revelation of the play of economic forces in his time and country. The experience of his childhood and youth in a farming community, where the peasant-workers were being subjected to an ever-increasing control by banks, railways, packers and other commercial and financial forces, was extended and strengthened by the spectacular development of organized finance in its handling of small and large manufacturing and commercial operations, which came into his view in the Chicago of the 'nineties. As he came to brood upon this growing domination of the wielders of pecuniary power over the industry of the country, and to perceive how this power came to penetrate and subdue to its offensive or defensive ends the educational system, to mould politics, and even to shape the reputable habits and conduct of social life, it was natural that his brand of economic determination of history should find expression in *The Theory of a Leisure Class* with its ironical yet substantially accurate account of the subtleties of the pecuniary domination.

But, though this economic *Lesson of the Day* continued to form an integral part of his teaching and was given later prominence in his *Engineers and the Price System*, it should not be taken as the final criterion of his intellectual value. It would, I think, not be difficult to show that this phase and force of pecuniary dominion, as evolved in the America of that generation, was not so wide or strong a factor in the capitalism of Europe and that even in America it was applicable in its full force to only a certain number of key industries. The effect of this doctrine of Veblen was, as we have seen, to over simplify the analysis of economic force in the distribution of wealth by assigning to a small body of pecuniary overlords the unearned or surplus wealth which Marx and other socialists imputed to capitalist employers and landlords. That this pecuniary control is of growing importance, alike in its control of industry, of commerce and of agriculture there can be no question, but its over-dramatization by Veblen cannot be taken as the real core of his contribution to sociology. It does, however, stand as the starting-point for his deep and powerful study of the psychological roots of our social system, as moulded by economic activities. For it was this early prepossession that drove him into his researches into the anthropological and psychological fields which more and more came to occupy his intellectual life. It is perhaps worthy of notice that the latest of his longer writings, *The Instinct of Workmanship*, is almost destitute of the satiric or sardonic humour which flavoured his earlier work, and stands out as an evident example of his serious absorption in dispassionate interpretation. It is here that we find the full historical and psychological account of the contrast and conflict between the workmanship disposition that survives in the technology of modern industry and the predatory disposition of the modern financial control. Nor does Veblen confine his analysis to the field of economics. As in his *Theory of a Leisure Class* he traced the influence of the economic conflict upon the political, religious, educational and other social institutions and activities of the present day, so here he finds an intricate relation at each stage in economic evolution from neolithic times, through barbarian and early handicraft to the beginnings of the Industrial Revolution, between the distinctively working life and the other interests and activities which help to make man's conscious career. As in his present-day analysis this relation between economic and non-economic factors is by no means a Marxist determinism, which gives complete supremacy and causative power to the former, but rather one of mutual interaction, so here he finds the instinct of workmanship in its continuous development from the most primitive arts and crafts to the highest terms of modern technology associated by give and take with the changes in politics religion and intellectual conditions. The history is by no means a smooth continuous process. Indeed, the story of economic and cultural changes set forth in this, the most erudite and subtly interpretative of Veblen's writings, is so compact that it is not possible to give a brief account that shall do justice to its intellectual power. Here we can only attempt to present the general course of its continuity.

His restless spirit of exploration drives Veblen back into pre-history in order to find the earliest co-operative play for the instinctive dispositions which enter into human workmanship and production. Though like other modern psychologists he recognizes the pitfalls attending the analysis of human motives, dispositions, activities into separable instincts, he refuses to dispense entirely with a term which within limits is indispensable. In speaking of a workman-like and a predaceous instinct, he insists that such instincts must have applied to them the terms conscious, social and

A SUMMARY AND ESTIMATE

teleological, or in other words that they imply a desire in the worker to do work which has a definite utility, a desire of the non-worker to win prestige by the forcible "getting something for nothing," i.e., the non-utility of his action.

This does not, however, signify that the end to which an instinct works is clearly perceived and kept in mind by the agent, still less that the ways and means he adopts under the prompting of an instinctive disposition are themselves instinctively adopted. "It is a distinctive mark of mankind that the working out of the instinctive proclivities of the race is guided by intelligence to a degree not approached by other animals.—Men take thought, but the human spirit, that is to say, the racial endowment of instinctive proclivities, decides what they shall take thought of, and how and to what effect."[1]

Among primitive men the interested spirit of workmanship is coupled with an attitude of mind towards the materials on which it works quite alien from the modern attitude. For all nature in some degree has an animism or anthropomorphism imputed to it, which carries a belief that some help or hindrance may come to man's work from the material on which it is employed. This applies more obviously to the organic material

[1] *The Instinct of Workmanship*, p. 6.

such as the animals and vegetables which carry within themselves independent powers of growth and decay. But the magic of primitive man, sustained, it would seem, by the relative ease or difficulty with which inorganic matter can be utilized for human ends, kept alive the imputation of animus to what we now call "dead matter." In other words, the inherent qualities of different sorts of materials seem to lend themselves to human purposes by some amenability or refractiveness that constitutes a spirit of their own. There is, however, as Veblen points out, this important difference in the anthropomorphic imputations as applied to organic and inorganic materials. In the former case the imputation is borne out by the conduct of the plants and animals themselves, exhibiting, as they do, inherent capacities of growth and change and compelling the human agent to activities that recognize and conform to those inherent capacities. In dealing with dead material any imputation of a directly animistic character is obstructive to technological advance, either by its misrepresentation of the facts and forces in question, or else by substituting magical or other irrational handling for the technical application of mechanical arts based upon a study of the properties of matter. Even when a belief in magic prevails, the power lies not in the material itself, but rather in the human agents who have access to magical methods.

A SUMMARY AND ESTIMATE

It was only by long experience in the details of workmanship that this habituation of attitude was weakened and yielded to a distinctively matter-of-fact objective treatment of the materials. That definitely scientific attitude towards workmanship is, indeed, even among advanced peoples, a comparatively modern acquisition. Nor does the animism which it displaced disappear from the human mind. It is pushed more and more into the widening background. "So an animistic conception of things comes presently to supplement and in part supplant, the more *naïve* and immediate imputation of workmanship, leading up to further and more elaborate myth-making; until in the course of elaboration and refinement there may emerge a monotheistic and providential Creator seated in an infinitely remote but ubiquitous space of four dimensions."[1] "It is as the creative workman, the Great Artificer, that he has taken his last stand against the powers of spiritual twilight."[2]

The dismissal of this animism from the details of workmanship, though conducive to a more practical as well as a more "scientific" attitude, is not, however, treated entirely as a gain. For just as an element of chance gives interest to an otherwise dull routine of repetition, so the element of initiation, left to the material on which man worked, served to provide the worker with some

[1] Op. cit., p. 59.   [2] Op. cit., p. 60.

sense of co-operation, strongest of course in agricultural work, with crops and herds, but not entirely absent from any technical industry.

But this aspect of what Veblen termed "Contamination of Instinct in Primitive Technology," is associated with others demanding delicate consideration. For the utility which is the more or less conscious end to which work is directed, though in its earliest form seemingly a directly personal utility (partly assisted, partly impeded, by the play of that instinct which Veblen terms "idle curiosity," the urge to seek knowledge for its own sake, the impulse towards disinterestedness understanding) comes to have a wider significance. Knowledge, thus acquired, may often be serviceable for workmanship and "can be digested for assimilation in a scheme of teleology that instinctively commends itself to the workmanlike sense of fitness. But it also follows that in so far as the personalized, teleological or dramatic order so imputed to the facts does not, by chance, faithfully reflect the causal relations subsisting among these facts, the utilization of them as technological elements will amount to a borrowing of trouble."[1] For "idle curiosity" is not merely the parent of disinterested science but also of imaginative interpretations which

[1] Op. cit., p. 89.

A SUMMARY AND ESTIMATE

may be as obstructive to such science as they are to technological utility. A definitely rational urge must not be imputed to what must be regarded rather as the "play" of human consciousness, the employment of the surplus energy of mind, placed at man's disposal after the fulfilment of the work biologically necessary for direct survival. Such surplus may flow into science or into the imaginative arts, including religion, decoration or "sports." In the long run this idle curiosity may, perhaps must, be regarded as the supreme source of human progress, supplying that ferment of risk-taking and experimental audacity without which habituation would keep humanity at a standstill, or place any step of progress in workmanship at the mercy of some chance handling or some environmental change.[1]

[1] How far is curiosity a separate instinct, urge or inclination? and in what sense is it "idle"? are two questions to which Veblen has not, I think, given sufficient attention. They are perhaps best approached through the conception of "play," the play of animals and of children. The approaches of most young animals to their environment is of a tentative experimental character in which curiosity is tempered with a caution that easily passes into fear. There is also some imputed animism. It is generally admitted by psychologists that such curiosity and its play are not essentially "idle," but have a biological survival value, both as affording a basis of security and ease in dealing with the immediate environment and in educating a skill and aptitude for future activities needed for getting food and protection. But the curiosity and accompanying play of animals have a purely static utility. They do not lead them to progress in the art of life, whereas man's curiosity is the chief instrument of his progress—its utility is definitely dynamic. But in what sense then can it be designated "idle"? Only in that its serviceability is not immediate. The curiosity of an infant or young child is not to be distinguished from that of a cat or a dog; it employs its several senses

The fact that man is "a social animal" has also an important bearing upon the instinct of workmanship. For even when a man is doing his own work in his own way, his consciousness of the product as an end or object, carries some social feeling. In the most primitive society the family is a close group, and his work must carry some sense of family utility. When division of labour, based on natural advantages of soil or

upon its immediate animate or inanimate environment, partly, apparently, from a mere physical craving to employ its limbs and senses, partly in order to discover what it can do with pleasure and safety. The "novelty" of sensation from such experimentation is clearly a source of pleasure, which, however, easily passes into fear or pain when impediments present themselves. This infantile play also has the utility imputed to the play of other animals: it furnishes practice of the limbs and senses for useful activities in later life. The curiosity attached to such play is, therefore, only "idle" in so far as its utility may be remote in time, and not confined to survival ends. This is more evidently true of adult curiosity. But when psychologists seek to make it a separable instinct and to give it a purely intellectual significance, they go beyond their brief. If instincts, urges, dispositions, are accorded a separate existence, even for purposes of linguistic convenience, the play aspect, with its "idle" curiosity, must be assigned to each instinct as a necessary part of its equipment. To claim that man alone is endowed with this additional instinct, urge or faculty, places the claimant in the difficulty of showing when and how in "the ascent of man" from his animal ancestry this instinct is inserted in his outfit.

Some defenders of the epithet "idle" may contend that it signifies not an absence of purpose but the application of purpose to the attainment of the higher values which mark out man from other animals. In this contention there is, of course, an element of truth. Though youthful curiosity is employed as other animals employ it for purposes of definitely survival value, it comes later to be employed for ends which are not "survival" but progressive in their nature, to feed the intellectual, spiritual and artistic, creative activities of which man alone is capable. But even so, it remains doubtful whether this higher nature of man implies that its origin in "idle curiosity" is a separate instinct or urge and not a composition of the various sorts of "play" in which the several instinctive faculties indulge on their own account.

A SUMMARY AND ESTIMATE

situation, and upon diversity of human aptitudes, begins to develop processes of barter or exchange, and little markets begin to appear, it is manifest that the sense of workmanship will be affected by the feeling of social utility in a wider than the family sense. Still more important, there will come a regard for "public opinion," the opinion first, of fellow-workers and next of other members of the community, in keeping an individual workman "up to the mark," and in giving credit and prestige for the good quantity and quality of his work.

Thus three distinguishable interests come to be attached to workmanship. The first is the pleasure derived from the activity itself, differing of course, widely with the kind of activity. In some activities there *is* a natural rhythm, as in the sweep of a scythe, the hauling of a rope, even the use of the spade, when the harsh muscular strain is relieved by a change of the muscles engaged, or by a periodic easing of the strain. In the fine arts of the dance and music this rhythmic factor in the use of organs is a positive sense of the physical pleasure attending such activities, creative or imitative, but even when the work is largely of a routine character inspired by the desire for a useful end, the play-rhythm may furnish a pleasurable "relief." Veblen has commented upon the loss involved under the inhuman rhythm of machinery of this relief element in work where the pace and order remain under human control.

The second source of satisfaction is the sense of the utility of workmanship. This is not wholly, or even primarily, a social feeling, perhaps not even a clearly selfish regard for a gainful end. The positive satisfaction in an emerging utility, due to one's skilful handling of materials, is best appreciated from the contrasted disgust at futility when no useful end is obtained. The felt utility must exceed the felt cost, or painful effort, in order that work may carry satisfaction. This satisfaction is perhaps not distinguishable from what Veblen terms "the sense of serviceableness," whether the service is to oneself, one's family, or some wider social group.

While the third source of satisfaction, the prestige element, cannot be regarded as a quality inherent in workmanship but rather as a pleasurable by-product, it certainly helps to evoke and sustain good workmanship, and must be taken into account in the net economy of a working life. But, so far as this prestige implies personal exploit in the sense of a competitive superiority over other workers, it begins to trench upon the predaceous instinct and is tinged with sadism. Such a statement does not, of course, dispose of the social utility claimed to proceed from "healthy

A SUMMARY AND ESTIMATE

competition" as evocative of skill and energy. But it illustrates at an early stage of the industrial arts the subtle nature of what Veblen calls "the contamination of workmanship" by alien motives.

The emergence of private ownership and property from simple primitive economy is a slow and uncertain process. For though the materials, tools and the knowledge and skill, needed in workmanship, belong to the workman, the modern sense of rights of property does not yet emerge in any clear feeling. "As determined by the state of the industrial arts in such a culture, the members of the community co-operate in much of their work to the common gain and to no one's detriment, since there is substantially no individual, or private gain to be sought. There is substantially no bartering or hiring, though there is a recognized obligation in all members to lend a hand, and there is, of course, no price, as there is no property and no ownership, for the sufficient reason that the habits of life under these circumstances do not evoke such a habit of thought."[1]

Here Veblen carries us back to the earliest stages of economic life. He discusses at length the claim that such a social condition is prior to anything that can be termed a predatory culture. Though predatory tendencies may be and are

[1] Op. cit., p. 143.

traceable in the weapons and the myths of primitive man, and though predatory eras occur in the history of most countries, the inherent survival value, the physical necessity of peaceful productive industry, gives to workmanship a strength and continuity denied to the life of war and plunder. The difficulties arising from this view in its bearing on early European history are frankly admitted. The dolico-blond stock on which modern industrial development has chiefly drawn, has commonly been regarded as possessed of a pugnacious and predatory temper to a larger extent than the other European stocks, and the problem arises how the peoples who were the most formidable disturbers of the peace of Europe for many centuries have come to be the most successful practitioners of modern technology and industry. To some extent this change-over may be attributed to a crossing of this stock by other racial stocks, thus tempering the predatory restlessness of the Northern blonds, and drawing their spirit of adventure into more gainful paths, first of commerce then of industry. In other words, the opportunities and fields of exploitation have shifted, and as there are few in any community to whom a life of war and plunder appeal as a lasting career, so the prestige of conspicuous wealth has co-operated with other political and social circumstances partly to sublimate, partly to displace the cruder predatory instinct of the dolicoblond peoples. This, of course, accords with his analysis both of the medieval economy and of later industrialism. The great predatory empires of the East with their unbridled despotisms and and their slavish populations, where the industrial arts suffered permanent paralysis and "civilization" was sterilized, were not found practicable in Europe. Even the great Roman Empire was not empire in a centralized despotic sense, and so far as it furnished an arena of military exploitation was comparatively short-lived. The Feudal System in which class-dominion and exploitation lasted some centuries, though coming within the category of predaceous rule, never developed a tyranny comparable with the Eastern tyrannies, either in its suppression of personal liberty or in its centralized organization. It did, however, produce a period known as the Dark Ages in which agriculture, the handicrafts, and commerce were crippled in development, and where internecine strife sucked up all the available surplus wealth beyond a bare and precarious maintenance for the under-populations. Not until the migration of more enterprising workers into towns and the establishment of a guild system, making it desirable for great Barons to afford liberty of work and life in return for serviceable loans and taxes, did industry regain some of the freedom necessary for technical advances.

Though the beginning of the subjugation of free workmanship to property and ownership goes back into remote prehistoric times,[1] wherever technological advance has yielded a considerable surplus income above the subsistence of the worker, and the material equipment of appliances (crops, fruit-trees, livestock, mechanical contrivances) renders outside surveillance and control possible, ownership vested chiefly in kingly or priestly power began to distinguish itself from workmanship. This early growth of predatory practice had its natural influence upon the sense of ownership. "Whatever may be conceived to have been the genesis of ownership, the institution is commonly found, in the barbaric culture to be tempered with a large infusion of predatory concepts, of status, prerogative, differential respect of persons and economic classes and a corresponding differential respect of occupations."— "The increase in industrial efficiency due to a sufficient advance in the industrial arts gives rise to the ownership of property and to pecuniary appreciation of men and things, occupations and products, habits, customs, usages, observances, services and goods. At the same time, since predation and war-

[1] Op. cit., p. 149.

A SUMMARY AND ESTIMATE

like exploit are intimately associated with the facts of ownership through its early history—there results a marked concentration of the self-regarding sentiments; with the economically important consequence that self-interest displaces the common good in man's ideals and aspirations."[1]

It was not, however, until the destruction or collapse of Feudalism in Europe and the beginnings of a National State that the economic class-system with its differentiation of ownership and workmanship began to assume its modern shape. That shape was due to the rise of a middle class, not predatory in the cruder sense of that word, "middle" not merely in income and ownership, but in its relation to an upper land-owning class and a lower working class. This middle class was primarily a business body, controlling and organizing workers for productive purposes and sometimes providing materials and tools, and marketing the product for its gainful ends. They formed the beginnings of a competitive system when the market area grew with improved communications. Out of their activities upon the European continent, especially in the Low Countries and South Germany, arose great specialized commercial ports handling international trade, while the beginnings of a money-lending power, like the Fuggers, came into brief prominence, to be swept away with the general collapse

[1] Op. cit., p. 160.

of trade and industry due to the dynastic struggles which soon ravaged the Northern Continent, reduced its populations to destitution, checked all technological advance, and brought to bankruptcy the early financiers.

Though Britain had been behind the Northern Continent both in industrial and commercial development, this break-back into predatory barbarism gave her an opportunity to forge ahead. Her insular position served to keep her out of foreign embroilments, at any rate so far as the mass of her people were concerned. She was an extensive borrower from the more advanced technical arts of the Continent, both for inventions and for skilled operatives, and though she did not take the leadership in the discovery and exploitation of the New World, European troubles enabled her to reap the fruits of the Spanish, Dutch and Italian adventures, while her growing sea-power began that process of quiet colonial acquisition which was to grow into a great world-empire.

It was the growing population and expanding home and foreign trade of Britain during this final period of handicraft that enabled and compelled her to take precedence in that economic transformation known as the Industrial Revolution. One phase of this revolution preceded the era of machinery and power. From the sixteenth century onward a business moneyed-class had been taking an ever-larger place in the organization of workmanship and the supply of materials in certain staple industries, chiefly for textile work. The actual work right up to the nineteenth century was mostly done within the home, though the previous century showed a strong tendency towards factories, where the beginnings of machine production were established. Steam-power, displacing human effort and skill in the use of tools, was the revolutionary change, for it made the worker the servant instead of the master of his tools and materials. The breach between ownership and workmanship became absolute with an accompanying loss of personal economic liberty for the proletariat.

The new situation is thus summarized by Veblen:—"(a) It is a competitive system: that is to say it is a system of pecuniary rivalry and contention which proceeds on stable institutions of property and contract, under conditions of peace and order. (b) It is a price system, i.e., the competition runs in terms of money, and the money unit is the standard measure of efficiency and achievement; hence competition and efficiency are subject to a rigorous accountancy in terms of a (putative) stable money unit. (c) Technologically the situation is dominated by the mechanical industries; so much so that even the costs of husbandry have latterly taken on much of the character of the mechanic acts. (d) Hence consumption is also standardized, proximately in mechanical terms of consumable products but, finally, through the mechanism of the market, in terms of price. (e) The typical industries which set the pace for productive work for competitive gains—and for competitive consumption, are industries carried on on a large scale; that is to say they are such as to require a large material equipment. (f) This material equipment—industrial plant and natural resources—is held in private ownership, with negligible exceptions.[1] (g) Technological knowledge and proficiency is in the main held and transmitted pervasively by the community at large; but it is also held in part by specially trained classes and individual workmen. Relatively little is in any special sense held by the owners of the industrial equipment, more especially not by the owners of typical large-scale industries. (h) It results that the owners of this larger material equipment, including the natural resources, have a discretionary control of the technological proficiency of the community at large. (i) In effect, therefore, the

---

[1] Here Veblen looks too exclusively at the United States, for in Britain and most Continental countries public ownership is far from "negligible" either in size or in the key character of the services it includes.

A SUMMARY AND ESTIMATE

owners of the necessary material equipment own also the working capacity of the community, and the usufruct of the state of the material arts."[1]

While this analysis restates more fully in some respects Veblen's central economic criticism of modern capitalism, to the effect that the pecuniary rulers of our economic system are so remote from the technicians, managers and workers who operate it, as to impede technological and managerial improvements from sheer ignorance, while their interests, which lie in profitable prices, are opposed to such increase of output as would come from the lower costs of technical advance, some confusion arises from the description of this economy as "competitive." For, so far as the pecuniary control of industry continues to be exercised by freely competing financial bodies, it is not easy to conceive how the deliberate policy of sabotage, upon which Veblen lays stress in his more specialized analysis, can take place. Where a monopoly of pecuniary interests is in control of a key industry or of the production of some necessary article of consumption, it may be profitable to curtail output so as to earn a larger net profit by maintaining a high price. But so far as free competition of productive businesses and their financial owners is maintained, or where monopoly is checked by the

[1] Op. cit., p. 220.

substitution of some article supplying the same need, sabotage, in the sense of deliberate limitation of output, would not be a profitable policy. In other statements of his central case Veblen seems clearly to recognize this situation and to impute the requisite monopoly control to his pecuniary power. Here, however, he bases his criticism upon the conflict between the knowledge of the producers (technicians and workers), and the technological ignorance of the financial owners, or "capitalists" in the modern sense of that term. "That the business community is so permeated with incapacity and lack of insight in technological matters is doubtless due proximately to the fact that their attention is habitually directed to the pecuniary issue of industrial enterprises; but more fundamentally and unavoidably it is due to the large volume and intricate complications of the current technological scheme, which will not permit any man to become a competent specialist in an alien and exacting field of endeavour, such as business enterprise, and still acquire and maintain an effectual working acquaintance with the state of the industrial arts."[1] The shareholders and the financial directors of great corporations admittedly cannot know much about the productive processes they control. But

[1] Op. cit., p. 224.

A SUMMARY AND ESTIMATE

need they be quite ignorant of their ignorance? No. In America an expert body of "efficiency engineers" has been developed as go-betweens, linking finance with the practical economy of production. Veblen, however, considers that the "efficiency" of these men is industrial only in a secondary degree, and that they are primarily devoted to the purpose of pecuniary gain. Indeed, the contamination of technical efficiency by the pecuniary motive is not confined to owners and their agents; it spreads among the "workers of all kinds and grades—labourers, mechanics, operatives, engineers, experts—all imbued with the same pecuniary principles of efficiency (who) go about their work with more than half an eye to the pecuniary advantage of what they have in mind."[1] That is to say, wages and salaries count for more than quality and quantity of productive activity in the minds of employees. That this is "natural" for workers whose work is mainly repetitive and machine-controlled may easily be conceded. But Veblen considers that it operates even upon the engineers and experts whose work carries qualities of inventive skill and enterprise. If so, it adds fresh difficulty to the social remedy which he has prescribed for the diseases of industry proceeding from pecuniary gainfulness. For that remedy consists,

[1] Op. cit., p. 346.

not, as according to the Marxist or other socialistic formulas, in placing organized society in ownership and control of the material and human factors of production, but in displacing the pecuniary control and vesting the whole ordering of industry in the engineers and technicians. Veblen would, however, presumably have met the difficulty here adduced by maintaining that the inherent qualities and human interests of workmanship, though damaged and impeded by the pecuniary invasion, still survived in their natural force and would respond to the appeal made to them by industrial reformers.

The main difficulty to any peaceful reformation along such lines is the habitual attitude of mind towards rights of property and individual ownership prevailing among all sections of the community. This attitude, sentimental and intellectual, is for Veblen a hold-over from the period when craftsmanship was the normal working method. In primitive times before skilled craftsmanship arose, the working life in a group or community was of a looser co-operative texture, with little either in the way of tools or of goods beyond the needs of current subsistence to form a fund of ownership. It was the subsequent era of craftsmanship that fastened a product upon the skilful activity of an individual worker, artificer or farmer, and evoked the sense of natural

A SUMMARY AND ESTIMATE

property in that which "he hath mixed his labour with." If he thus created a useful thing, it belonged to him by right and it was for him to consume it, use it, or convey it to his heir. Production was then essentially an individualistic process and individual property was the natural consequence. The laws and customs, gradually adopted and adapted to this economic era, became themselves "natural" and rational, and acquired a sort of sanctity attested by morals and fortified by religious precepts in a Protestantism which had broken away from the over-centralized authority of the Roman Church because of the insistent urge after self-government and individual direction in spiritual and temporal affairs. This mutual adaptation between individualism in the fields of economics and of religion, especially the stimulus afforded by the narrower Protestant creeds and Churches to the qualities of personal industry, thrift and far-sightedness which made for business success, has received close attention from the treatment of Weber, Tawney and others.

In his discussion of "The Era of Handicraft" Veblen makes an interesting commentary upon the changes in religious faith and feeling which were brought about, not by deliberate reflection but by a natural adjustment to the new working routine of life which displaced the servility of feudalism.

"A change," he says, "passed over the spirit of theological speculation, whereby the fundamentals of the faith were infused with the spirit of the handicraft system, and the presumptions of workmanship insensibly supplanted those of mastery and subservience in the working concepts of devout Christendom."—"God had not ceased to be the Heavenly King and had not ceased to be glorified with the traditional phrases of homage as the Most High, the Lord of Hosts, etc., but somewhat incongruously He had also come to be exalted as the Great Artificer—the preternatural craftsman. The vulgar habits of thought bred in the workday populace by the routine of the workshop and the market-place had stolen their way into the sanctuary and the counsels of divinity."[1]

This change in the conception of the operative function of the Deity was accompanied by a moral and religious individualism which brought each man into personal relation with God, dispensing with the offices of the Church as authorized middleman or reducing them to the position of subsidiary aids to the religious life.

But Veblen is mainly concerned with the effects of habituation in an individualism which, though adapted to useful procedure in its time of origin, is wholly inappropriate to a period from which personal craftsmanship has virtually disappeared

[1] Op. cit., p. 257.

A SUMMARY AND ESTIMATE

and where products can no longer be regarded as the creation of individual owners or workers. The difficulty of getting either the legal owners of modern productive resources, or the common sense of the community to perceive that the change from craftsmanship to capitalism and from early capitalism to pecuniary capitalism, requires a corresponding change in thought and sentiment regarding rights of property and the control of industry, is for him the gravest problem of our time. For unless some process of education can with reasonable rapidity bring both the present economic ruling class, the engineers and the proletariat, to methods of pacific reform, resort will be had to force, either by the workers, in order to capture a system so essential to their well-being but in the control of which they have no part, or by the owning class in defence of the legal rights which they still maintain to be their natural and moral rights. What has occurred in Russia, in Germany and Italy, seems to bear testimony to this peril, confirming the fears which Veblen entertained. That the pecuniary ownership which vests control in men out of intelligent effective contact, either with the managers or the workers of the businesses they own, can continue to operate in waste, price-fixing and unemployment, as it does at present, is beginning to seem socially indefensible to thinking minds irrespective of their political, class, or moral affinities.[1] It is possible that a piece-meal graduation which shall reconcile increasing public ownership, or control of key industries, with a taxing system which shall transfer to social services the bulk of any profitable surplus that may accrue to private concerns better left to individual enterprise, may achieve a peaceable revolution in such capitalist countries as Britain and the United States. But the tough survival of natural rights of private personal property into an economic epoch for which it becomes continually more unsuited stands as the most critical problem of our time. It cannot be solved peacefully and successfully without changes in our attitude of mind which shall involve corresponding reforms in all our institutions and valuations. The term valuation is

[1] Veblen did not live to see the fulfilment of his prophetic vision of American economic life after 1929. At first sight it might have seemed that the distinctively financial collapse of 1929–30 indicated the failure of the pecuniary oligarchy to keep their power over the industrialists and "engineers." For the banks in most parts of the country showed no resisting power to the wave of depression and the investors and depositors were subjected to ruinous losses. Bad as were the conditions of most industrial undertakings with their idle plant and unemployed workers, the paralysis of pecuniary business seemed worse. But when recovery is brought about, whether by natural or artificial processes, it will probably be found that the New Deal has strengthened the financial control over the economic system, partly by consolidation of the banking system through the elimination of numerous feeble local banks, partly by the devising of processes by which public credit shall be placed behind the private banks without embarking on any un-American system of national ownership.

A SUMMARY AND ESTIMATE

perhaps the most significant. For the transformation of an ownership based on individual productivity to one based on pecuniary accountancy not merely raises the above-named issues of social waste and moral defectiveness. It corrodes the very meaning of civilization by the insistence on a quantitative calculus, applied in mechanistic terms to human workmanship and its products. Nobody denies the utility of money as a measure and a medium of exchange, but the place it has assumed in the thoughts, feelings and activities of mankind is out of keeping with any sane conception of human progress. By seizing and narrowing to its purely quantitative purpose the meaning of such terms as "value," "worth" and "wealth," it has exercised a noxious influence upon all those finer arts which go to the refinement of personality and humanity. The effect of this abuse is seen not merely in the science of economics by the expulsion of all ethical conception of ends and by the reduction of all qualitative vital costs and satisfactions to standard measurements. For economic science this pressure towards mathematical exactitude may seem desirable. But when such a science takes upon itself to give authoritative direction to the arts of industry and commerce, its disregard of qualitative differences becomes a vital peril. For the assumption that quantitative values are, by reason of the choice exercised by producers and consumers, a substantially correct criterion of human costs and satisfactions, ignores some salient truths of modern industry and commerce, and any national economy based on this assumption is doomed to waste and sterility. And when, as is everywhere the case, such a quantitative economics exerts influence upon the politics of a nation either in its internal or its external rule, it fosters class-strife and international strife. For the pecuniary measure of wealth and value is bound to regard both personal and national success in terms of quantitative competition, reverting to the invidious predatory temper of pre-craftsmanship, in which one man's or one class's or one nation's gain is another man's, another class's, another nation's loss.

Ruskin rightly fastened upon the corruption of the word "value" as the index of an unjust and wasteful industry, involving the impossible task of reducing qualitative to quantitative differences. So far as qualitative considerations enter into productive powers and resources, progress consists in increasing the proportion of such powers and resources as are put to the production of non-routine goods which go to meet the higher and more individual needs and satisfactions. A purely pecuniary accountancy in which numbers of population, size of incomes, rate of growth of commercial values, are the items of measurable success, takes no account of this vital progress. Yet there is a general acceptance of this pecuniary valuation and of the individualistic sense of ownership which goes with it, as an inheritance of the era of craftsmanship—which it has displaced. Such, Veblen holds, is the result of carrying over by habituation the natural conceptions of craftsmanship into the discordant atmosphere of modern large-scale mechanical industry with its pecuniary rule. The individualism, the natural rights of property, the personal management of the older era are all alien from the modern economy. But the pretence of their existence and the sentiments attaching to them still cling to the mentality not merely of the possessing classes but of the majority of workers. Indeed, as regards the working classes, the false individualism of the doctrine that a worker is robbed of the bulk of the product of his personal labour forms a common and injurious factor in his "rights of labour" and the sort of "socialism" which it inspires. But, speaking generally, the stubborn adherence to an antiquated individualism, in the belief that the owner of property has made its pecuniary value, or has received it from one who has made it, remains a firm rock of resistance for the propertied classes against the claims of the workers and of the community.

How far this clinging to obsolescent ideas of natural rights, creative initiative and individualism can survive when their intellectual supports have been undermined by the accepted modern theories of causation, conservation of energy, and evolution, converting nature into a regular mechanical process in accordance with the workaday teaching of the modern industrial arts, is a question to which Veblen gives no clear answer. This is not his fault. He can only set the issue in such light of current experience as falls within his vision. He recognizes that in general the intellectual classes have brought their thinking into conformity with the teaching of modern science and the mechanical conception of causation which it adopts, expelling from their consideration all theological or other creative happenings that conflict with the quantitative continuity of energy which is the basic conception of this science. This attitude is easy of acceptance by ordinary practical men whose work, indeed, assumes and demonstrates this continuity. Persisted in, it must, he thinks, gradually supersede the creative sense and sentiment of the earlier craftsmanship with the religious, legal and political supports on which it rested. Such a process,

A SUMMARY AND ESTIMATE

however, may be very slow. Harsh as has been the discrepancy between the received system of economic institutions on the one side and the working of the machine technology on the other, its effect in reshaping current habits of thought in these processes has hitherto come to nothing more definitive than an uneasy conviction that "Something will have to be done about it."[1] Not only is there a reluctance to face up to the requirements of the new order as regards the sloughing of the antiquated scheme of business principles and the conduct of industrial affairs in accordance with recognized social needs alike of control and of distribution. There are also definite signs of attempts at an anti-scientific reversion to creative powers, a "recrudescence of magic, occult science, telepathy, spiritualism, vitalism, pragmatism."[2] Veblen cites Bergson as a leader in this new anti-scientific trend of thought. There are, however, among scientists themselves, as we now see, as well as among philosophers, tendencies to a definite revolt against the determinism and the quantitative continuity of late-Victorian science. First comes the rejection of the conception of efficient causation as an unnecessary and therefore unwarranted assumption for scientific purposes; science can conduct

[1] Op. cit., p. 342.   [2] Op. cit., p. 334.

its processes on a basis of calculated probability. But this rejection of determinism does not suffice for our scientific divers into philosophy. Emergent evolution brings unpredictable novelties into the processes of history, and disorder, hazard, chance, are brought into the play of energetic action. Intuition is invoked as an independent source of information regarding the higher values, and reason is driven back to the Hobbes' condition of "a slave of the passions," i.e., an instrument for calculating the means of obtaining interested ends. Though this line of thought cannot rightly be regarded as a mere reversion to pre-scientific thinking, and cannot be relied upon to give support to obsolescent economic and political ideas and institutions, it does distinctly contravene the doctrines of mechanical causation in their moulding of modern thought and sentiment. Its emphasis upon novelty in evolutionary processes, and upon elements of chance constitutes a direct challenge to the logic of ordinary thought as well as to the determinist philosophy.

How far Veblen would have lent a favourable ear to this latest thinking as a substitution for the mechanical determinism that had displaced the craftsmanlike mentality, it is not possible to judge. But his evident sympathy with craftsmanship as the saner form of work would lead one to conjecture that his personal philosophy would lean towards a retention of the creative spirit of which craftsmanship was an economic expression. Though his brief occasional excursions into theology are concerned not with the truth or falsehood of its doctrines but with the part it plays as spiritual offspring of and assistant to the different social-economic forces, it might be expected that his stress upon the predatory character of the modern pecuniary dominion would evoke strong moral reprobation. But though his analyses of predatory processes with their "something for nothing," their profitable bargains based on economic force, their sabotage of technical productivity, their seizure of the social inheritance of economic knowledge and opportunity for their own profitable ends—though these practices would seem to warrant grave ethical condemnation, Veblen for the most part abstains from any formal condemnation and leaves his readers to make their own moral commentary. The posthumous volume of Essays does, however, contain one interesting article[1] upon "Christian Morals and the Competitive System" in which he contrasts directly Christian morals and business principles as "the institutional

[1] Reprinted from *The International Journal of Ethics*, Vol. XX, January, 1910.

by-products of two different cultural situations. The distinctive qualities of the former are taken to be non-resistance (humility) and brotherly love while the latter are the egoistic rights and liberties of the individual in an era of pecuniary transactions. A sort of compromise between the two codes is found in the principle of 'fair play' the nearest approach to 'the Golden Rule' that the pecuniary civilization will admit."[1] But, though admitting both that the principles of fair play have lost the sanction afforded by the human propensity for serviceability to the common good, and that "There is little in the current situation to keep the natural right of pecuniary discretion in touch with the impulsive bias of brotherly love," Veblen ends upon a more hopeful note, to the effect that "the ancient racial bias embodied in the Christian principle of brotherhood should logically continue to gain ground at the expense of the pecuniary march of competitive business."[2]

· · · · ·

This judgment finds support from two sources that receive prominent attention in Veblen's teaching. One is the persistent undermining of that sense of the right of individual property, which belonged to the age of personal craftsman-

[1] *Essays in our Changing Order*, p. 215.   [2] Op. cit., p. 218.

A SUMMARY AND ESTIMATE

ship, by the substitution of a series of productive processes so essentially co-operative that the very notion of a single worker making any final product by his own effort became unthinkable. The "natural" right of property in that which a man has himself made thus disappears. The other ethical support is found in the self-defeating character of the pecuniary power, forced in what appears to be its profit-making interest, to practise a sabotage of productivity. Since the logic of this process must continually intensify a process directly and obviously hostile to the interests alike of producers and consumers, there must come a time when the intensity of this hostility will find active expression in the repudiation of a pecuniary despotism so injurious to every form of personal security and economic progress.

. . . . .

It would not be right to consider this account of the services rendered by one of the most brilliant, independent and penetrative minds of our age without some brief comment upon two matters that bear upon the author as an exponent of sociology. One is the question of his mode of expression, the other of the applicability of a distinctively American critique to the wider field of present-day civilization. These two questions are not unrelated. His *Theory of the Leisure Class* gained many readers but probably suffered loss of serious intellectual attention because of a pervasive tone of irony conveyed in part by linguistic formalities. Though this was in a degree characteristic of most, though by no means all, of his writings, its prominence in the earliest of his books served to give him a reputation for humour which, though in some ways protective, postponed and even damaged his legitimate reputation as the keenest social thinker of his time. He did not deliberately choose and cultivate this humorous attitude. It was inherent in the social situation as he saw it. His approach was throughout that of an interested onlooker, seeking to understand the spectacle of American life. Now life, it has been said, is a comedy to those who think, a tragedy to those who feel. The saying certainly contains a large element of truth. For the thinker must adopt the impartial spectatorial position so far as he can. Now Veblen's early years of detachment from the main current of American life undoubtedly helped him to maintain an attitude of critical aloofness. His later experiences gave him a wide knowledge of social facts and tendencies without immersing him in the sensational romance of American life. This enabled him to give novel and surprising

A SUMMARY AND ESTIMATE

exhibitions and interpretations of situations, occurences and valuations, which by the ordinary American were accepted as normal, natural and calling for no explanation. So far as those phenomena came under ordinary survey they seemed to belong to a social order that was essentially equitable and rational, because equity and reason were taken for granted in "the best of all worlds." Now to such a mentality the revelations of psychology, either personal or social, must always carry an element of sudden surprise—the basic element of all humour. When Veblen, therefore, showed how the interests of the economic masterclass drew into its gainful course, by half-conscious or subconscious methods of attraction, the controls of politics, religion, culture, recreation, social prestige, that could give assistance an protection to its business methods, the unmasking of such a relation between presumably independent activities and institutions was essentially humorous. A merely rational exposure of such secret "goings on" carried an ironical flavour which was strengthened by a formal terminology and an avoidance of all emphatic forms of condemnation. Indeed, there was nearly always in Veblen's account of what might appear flagrant acts of folly or injustice a note of meiosis, which though not common in American humour (for this tends towards exaggeration), aroused a subtler sense of comedy. This element in Veblen's writings does not imply either that he was devoid of sympathy for suffering and of indignation at the folly or injustice of the perpetration of such wrongs, or that he deliberately committed himself to cold irony as a literary method. To all who knew him the style was inseparable from the man, his natural mode of expression.

How far this method of expression and the substance of its social revelation are fully applicable to the wider world situation is a question to which no confident answer is possible. Though much of Veblen's research into social history from primitive times is drawn from non-American sources (especially his investigations into racial characteristics and the earlier contrasts of the working and the predatory life), his analysis of the dominion of pecuniary interests over industry, the relations between "engineers and the price system," the supremacy of quantitative over qualitative values extending into the fields of education, religion and art, is peculiarly American. In economic life this means that capitalism both in its competitive and its combinative processes has been there less hampered by political and legal controls, and by humanitarian sentiments and customary curbs than in most European countries.

A SUMMARY AND ESTIMATE

Indeed, it has thriven upon the prevailing beliefs that America is the land of equal opportunity open to all industrious citizens, and that free individual institutions and enterprises are still the open gates to a serviceable and laudable personal career. The experience of the falsity of these presumptions was followed in Veblen's writings by industrious and diverting researches into the methods of economic determinism by which the presumptions helped to mould all other social activities and institutions. As applied to capitalist countries of Europe these sharp methods of analysis, though essentially true, would be blurred by many qualifying and even counteracting motives and movements less active in the United States. The organization of pecuniary control, as distinct from industrial management, has there not gone so far and has in many of the key industries been checked and mitigated by State ownership or regulation. Though law and the administration of justice everywhere carry heavy burdens of property rights and inequalities that count against the equal freedom of the under-classes, the gross corruption that prevails in America is less prevalent in most European countries. The development of public social services, outside the educational field, and the taxing system in its incidence on rents, profits and other "surplus" elements of income (though damaged by the recent growth of taxation upon working-class consumption), the increased public expenditure upon housing and other working-class benefits, have tended both to limit the area of pecuniary dominion and to move towards a larger social utilization of surplus income. Such considerations, however, do not impair the essential soundness of Veblen's central analysis, alike in its direct economic and its indirect social bearings upon the modern course of development in all countries advanced in their industrial and financial methods. Recent world-history assigns a definitely determinant place to the organized will of dominant economic power in the arts of war and peace, not in the sense that other non-economic influences, such as power, prestige and territorial greed may not in some cases possess more potent direct causative influence, but because the greater persistence and foresight of acute business men can and do best utilize these other non-economic forces for their gainful policies. It is the impressive manner in which Veblen has expounded this form of economic determination of history and traced its resulting influence upon other human activities and institutions that establishes his claim to rank as one of the great sociologists of our time.

INDEX

A

American Economics Association, 15
American Federation of Labour, 128
Animism, 24, 187, 189
Arts and Crafts, 100

B

Blond, Dolico, 196
Boer War, 143
Böhm-Bawerk, 16
Bryan, William Jennings, 136

C

Catholic Church, 157
Cairnes, 34
Carleton College, 12, 14
Chase, Stuart, 21
China, 146
Churches, 158
Clark, Prof. J. B., 14, 46 f.
Class Distinctions of, 180
Classical Theory, 44
Constitution, Federal, 127
Cost Theory, 41 f.
Curiosity, 191; idle, 190

D

Darwinism, 62
Davenport, H. J., 18
Determinism, Repudiation of, 27

Dial, The, 19 f.
Dogs, 163
Dorfman, Joseph, 10 (Quoted in Chap. 1 and passim)
Dress, Prestige in, 176 f.

E

Education, The Economics of, 104 ff.; Financial Control of, 120
Ely, Prof. Richard, 15
Employments, Gradation of, 86
"Engineers", 134
Engineers and the Price System, 184
Equivalence, Doctrine of, 45

F

Fashion, Novelty in, 99
Feudal System, 197, 199
Finance in Education, 116; in Politics, 124 ff.
Fuggers, the, 199

G

Gambling, 169
Germany, Imperial, 143, 148
George, Henry, 15

H

Hedonism, Repudiation of, 37, 50

INDEX

Hitler, 137
Hobbes, 216
House, Colonel, 19
Humour in Veblen, 221
Hunting, 168

I

"Idle Curiosity", 23, 108 ff.
Imperial Germany, 140
Imperialism, Lenin's, 129
Individualism in America, 163
Industrial Revolution, 28, 185, 200
Instinct of Workmanship, 185, 187
Investment, 122

J

Jordan, David Starr, 17

K

Kelmscott Press, 100

L

Laski, Harold, 85
Laughlin, Prof. J. L., 16
League of Nations, 147, 150
Leisure, Conspicuous, 94 ff.
Leisure Class, Theory of the, 87 ff.
Leland Stanford University, 17

M

Magic, 169
Manners, 93

Marginalism, 41
Marginal Utility, 46
Marshall, Alfred, 34
Marx, Attitude towards, 53
Mechanization, 30; of Mind, 31 f.
Mill, J. S., 34 f.
Monte Carlo, 170
Morris, William, 100
Motor-Car, 173
Mussolini, 137

N

Nature of Peace, Chap. vii
Nation, The, 19
Nationalism, Economic, 139, 152, 154
Neutralization, 147
New Jersey, 127
New Republic, 19
New School for Social Research, 20

O

Opportunity, Equality of, 128
Ownership, Prestige of, 91; Sense of, 198

P

Peace, The Nature of, 130 ff.
Play, 167
Politics, the Field of, 121
Predatory Nature, 89, 92
Prestige, Personal, 164 ff.
Price System, 51
Property, Regard for, 90
Protestantism, Spirit of, 156

INDEX

R

Rent, 40
Rhodes, Cecil, 143
Ricardo, 39
Rights, Material, 214, 218
Roman Empire, 197
Rosebery, Lord, 117
Russia, 20, 64, 209

S

Sabotage, Charge of, 76, 132
Savings, 70
Smith, Adam, 34, 37
Socialism, The Theory of, 53
Socialism, Veblen's, 66 ff.
  Wartime, 129
Sombart, 17
Spencer, Herbert, 16
Sport, 168, 171
Standard Oil Trust, 72, 126
Standardization, 118
Steffens, Lincoln, 126
Surplus, 52

T

Tawney, 207
Taxonomics, 43
Technology, 21, 27
Theology, Changes in, 208
Trade Unions, 63

U

United Steel Corporation, 73
Universities, State, 111; Control of, 114

V

Value, 212
Veblen, Thorstein: Early Years, 12; Carleton College, 12; Madison, 14; Yale, 15; Cornell, 15; Marriage, 15; Chicago University, 16; *The Theory of the Leisure Class*, 16; Leland Stanford, 17; *The Higher Learning in America*, 18; Columbia University, 18; *Imperial Germany*, 18; *The Nature of Peace*, 19; edits *The Dial*, 19; *The Vested Interests*, 19; New School for Social Research, 20; *Absentee Ownership*, 21, 79; *The Place of Science*, Ch. II; *The Preconceptions of Economic Science*, 33
Virtue, 165, 174

W

Ward: *Pure Sociology*, 17
Weber, 207
Wicksteed, Philip, 41